Niranjan Seshadri and Erika Seshadri live on an animal rescue ranch in Sarasota, Florida, with their three children. In their fleeting moments of spare time, they enjoy writing poetry together. Niranjan's penchant for adventure and Erika's love of writing provided the perfect storm in which to create their debut work, *Himalayan Tsunami.*

For Dad and Appa.

Niranjan Seshadri and Erika Seshadri

HIMALAYAN TSUNAMI

AUSTIN MACAULEY PUBLISHERS™

LONDON • CAMBRIDGE • NEW YORK • SHARJAH

A CIP catalogue record for this title is available from the British
Library.

ISBN 9781528968911 (Paperback)
ISBN 9781528969550 (ePub e-book)

www.austinmacauley.com

First Published 2023
Austin Macauley Publishers Ltd®
1 Canada Square
Canary Wharf
London
E14 5AA

This book was born through the existence, encouragement, and support of innumerable human beings. We'd like to thank everyone who has been along on this great journey with us in any form or fashion, especially:

Our parents, friends, and family who have believed in us from the get-go;

Our biggest fans—Anjali, Adrian, and Ajay;

Om Swami, for your invaluable mentoring and friendship;

Nikki T, Chrissy W, and Colin B at Write My Wrongs Editing, whose services were magically impeccable;

Deborah Bradseth from Tugboat Design, for bringing artistic ideas to life;

Robin Corum, Jay Squires, and Liz O'Neil, for your investments of detailed feedback in the manuscript's early stages;

Chris Hardin of Hardin Bourke Entertainment, and Ed Kowalczyk of Live, for putting up with random bits of nonsense;

Reverend Lee Wolak, who is always up for another adventure; and

The incredible team at Austin Macauley Publishers, for making a dream come true.

Chapter 1

"Code blue, ER, Bay One!"

The call over the hospital speakers snapped me out of intense focus. I was in the final moments of an exacting heart procedure. An elderly man lay on the table, his fate to be decided by how steady I could keep my hands. I had inserted a wire into his circulatory system through an artery in his leg and was carefully threading it towards his heart. The X-ray enhancer hovering above his chest revealed the blockage that threatened his life. Powerful overhead lights illuminated the beads of sweat gathering along the edge of my surgical cap. I had one chance to get it right. With a flick of my wrist, I deployed a metallic mesh stent into my patient's main coronary artery.

"Twenty atmospheres. Up, and finally down," I said to the nurse who meticulously recorded minute-by-minute events from the control room. I glanced at the vital signs displayed on a large monitor. Half of the screen portrayed the heart as a pulsing shadow, and the other half offered the reassuring blip of a regular heartbeat. The blockage was open, allowing blood to flow back into his starving heart. Success.

"Music, please," I said to the nurse. I looked at my patient with affection, knowing he was a beloved father and doting grandpa. Sucking in a long breath, I allowed relief to settle deep into my lungs. A rich baritone voice from my portable stereo filled the sterile air with Beethoven's 'Ode to Joy'.

> *O Freunde, nicht diese Töne!*
> *Sondern laßt uns angenehmere anstimmen*
> *Und freudenvollere!*
> *O friends, not these sounds!*
> *But let's start with more pleasant ones*
> *And more joyful!*

It was impossible to hear Beethoven without thinking of my own father, who was over nine thousand miles away in Bangalore, India. During my childhood there, it was not unusual for him to spend hours at a time tucked away in his study, listening to Western classical music. Occasionally, I would join him. His analyses of various concertos and symphonies were always interesting to me. His love of music became apparent as a child the day my grandfather brought home a precious imported radio set. It sat enticingly in an ornate wooden box in the living room, but my grandfather forbade all of his seven kids to touch it. As a result, my father built his own homemade radio at the age of ten. I smiled at the thought of him, wondering if he was currently hearing the same music as I was.

"Code blue, ER, Bay One!" the call came again.

No one had answered the code. I whipped off my gloves and hurried to the hospital phone to call the ER. A frantic voice answered.

"Doctor, the patient is coding. Seventy-year-old male. We've shocked him six times. We're losing him."

I sprinted to the emergency room despite my exhaustion from being on call for seven days straight. The patient was in ventricular arrhythmia. If we couldn't get his heartbeat back to a normal rhythm within four minutes, his brain would start to die.

"Continue CPR." I raised my voice over the commotion. Years of experience allowed my nerves to remain calm while my mind raced to address the urgency of the situation. "Anyone not directly connected with this code, please exit."

Too many bodies were in motion around the room, consuming precious seconds.

"Give epinephrine, continue CPR, charge, and defibrillate," I ordered. The patient's irregular heartbeat persisted, suggesting he was the victim of a massive heart attack. There was no time to position a breathing tube in his airway. Instead, we placed the face mask of an Ambu bag over his nose and mouth, which allowed us to manually pump air into his lungs. The gurney's wheels spun wildly as we jogged down a long corridor to the cath lab's procedure room. I looked back at the ER to see a social worker quietly leading the patient's wife into a grief counselling room.

Once in the cath lab, my team of skilled staff worked as one fluid entity, anticipating every move I made. As a result, I was able to insert the wire and deploy the stent in record time. My patient had a type of blockage cardiologists refer to as the 'widow-maker'. Less than 15 percent of patients survive such a heart attack if it happens outside of a medical facility.

I retraced my steps through the long corridor towards the ER. The patient's wife sat crumpled in a chair, her eyes moist and a tissue clutched tightly in her small, bony fist. I sat down beside her, put my hand on hers, and smiled.

A sob escaped her frail body.

"He'll be fine," I said.

She opened her mouth to speak, but the words stuck in her throat. She nodded her head, fresh tears forging new paths down her cheeks. I explained how close we came to losing him.

"We've been married fifty years," she said, finding her voice again. "We just got back from a mission trip to Haiti. We were helping with the earthquake relief. If this had happened down there..."

I nodded, confirming her thought.

"Well, God was really looking out for us, wasn't He?" She hugged me tightly and whispered, "Thank you."

I felt elated by the outcome of that morning's cases. However, it was only 10:00 a.m. I still had a full day of unknowns ahead of me. The schedule of a cardiologist is highly unpredictable. Unlike a painful ankle, which can afford a wait-and-see approach, chest pain is too often a medical emergency. I live by the saying, "Time is muscle." The sooner someone receives treatment for a heart attack, the more likely they will make a full recovery. Once the heart becomes distressed, the countdown clock begins. Over those past months, I'd been on call so often my body was perfectly used to jolting awake in the middle of the night. I could gather my wits about me by the third ring of the phone and take less than thirty minutes to transport myself from the dark depths of dreamless sleep to the bright surgical lights of the cath lab.

I left the room and took a minute to collect my thoughts before things got hectic again. I'd been working so hard the past year or so that I couldn't remember the last time I'd been able to appreciate the simple beauty of a sunrise or sunset. Each day, I left home before dawn and returned again in darkness. Too many of my occasional glimpses of blue sky were through the hospital windows. I thought of my eternally patient wife, who had been caring for our kids all those months with little contribution from me. They were still too young to comprehend how much I was absent, but what about when they got older? I felt a pang of guilt as I thought of my second child. Though present for his birth, I was called away to work again immediately after. His entire infancy was a blur to me. I knew I was missing out on first steps and first words, and thinking about that burdened me with an overwhelming sense of loneliness. Had I chosen the right career? Was I saving lives at the cost of living my own?

My road to becoming a doctor began at age ten or eleven, a time in my life when I was my grandfather's second shadow. I accompanied him everywhere he went when I wasn't in school. He graduated from medical school in the late 1930s. He had hoped to study as an ENT specialist in Vienna, Austria, and eventually make his way to work in the United States. War clouds over Europe forced him to change his plans and stay in India, where he began a long, illustrious career as a general practitioner.

Though my grandfather's mission in life was to heal people, his obsession was tennis. I spent many days watching him play under sunny skies at the Bowring Sports Institute. He was always impeccably dressed in a white shirt and pants, which quite resembled Wimbledon's dress code at the time. After all, Bowring was an old country club left behind by the colonial British. One afternoon, he handed me his spare racket and instructed me to knock around a few tennis balls on the practice wall. He later suggested I start formal tennis lessons. I duly complied.

The following summer, Boris Becker won the Wimbledon championship for the first time at the age of seventeen. I remember watching the finals with my grandfather. He looked at me and said, "I have no hope of you making it as a professional tennis player. Look at Becker, where he is at this age, and where you are, just a few years behind. You can play for fun if you wish, but I want you to become a doctor like me, go to America, and make a life for yourself there." And so, thanks to Boris Becker's victory at Wimbledon, my life plan was set.

I'd always felt a great sense of accomplishment and fulfilment in being able to help so many people with my profession. Yet, running a solo physician practice for years while juggling so many roles day in and day out was wearing me down. Sometimes it made me question if it wasn't my dream I was living, but my grandfather's. At the end of one particularly challenging procedure, I found myself sitting alone in the windowless control room of the cath lab. Computer monitors flashed images undecipherable to the untrained eye while fatigue was trying its best to defeat me. Was that my grandfather's idea of success?

At that point, I could tell burnout was closing in on me. If I didn't somehow find a balance between work life and home life, I was going to become wholly miserable. I longed for an escape to reset my mind. I often wound down after work by watching documentaries of men and women brave enough to jump headlong into the unknown. I admired their strength and spirit when summiting the world's highest peaks or diving its deepest oceans. The recurring themes of adventure, self-discovery, and solitude woke something within me. Would I ever get the chance to experience something like that? Soon enough, the answer manifested itself in an email. I received notification of a meditation retreat deep in the heart of the Himalayas and knew it was the opportunity I'd been waiting for.

Late one night after a particularly difficult day, I turned down the long, winding driveway that led home to our little animal rescue ranch. A few lights were still on in the house. They offered a warm, welcoming glow through the windows—even if everyone else was asleep. I noticed, then, that all the lights were on in the barn. When I pulled up, it became apparent my wife was carrying an armload of medicine and bandages. *Which one of the animals is hurt?* I wondered. It could have been any one of our horses, sheep, dogs, cats, or tortoises.

"Hey!" I said, jumping out of the car. "Is everything okay?"

"Yeah, don't worry. I just need to soak and wrap Cowboy's hoof. He has an abscess."

I watched as she mixed Epsom salts into a bucket of warm water and gently picked up the horse's hoof, placing it into the solution. Then she stood there, her hand scratching his withers.

"What are you doing now?" I asked.

"Waiting. If I move, he'll pull his leg out. He's not very cooperative."

"How long do you have to stand there like that?"

"Twenty minutes. If no one wakes up." She pointed to the baby monitor sitting on the nearest bale of hay.

I decided it was the best time to tell her about the retreat.

"I want to go to the Himalayas."

Her right eyebrow perked up, as it always does after one of my sudden announcements. "Please don't tell me you want to relax by climbing a mountain."

"No, of course not." I laughed, pretending the thought had never crossed my mind. "I want to sign up for a two-week silent meditation retreat. It's in a remote part of the Himalayas, but no mountain climbing is required. I promise."

"That still sounds kind of dangerous. What's the elevation?"

"Oh, you know, not too high."

"Ha!" She snorted. "Tell me for real."

"I don't know, but it's not like I'm going to Everest."

"How are the roads up the mountain?"

"Uh… not too bad."

"Are you lying?"

"Probably."

"Ugh. Wouldn't it be easier to go somewhere in this country? You could do a nice Zen retreat in California or something. A short plane ride, safe roads…"

I could tell she was trying to be supportive, but worry was getting the best of her.

"What better place than the Himalayas, though?" I asked, hopeful she would agree. The mountains were a perfect mixture of rugged openness, spiritual energy, and strange familiarity. When I was growing up, my grandmother frequently told me alluring tales from the Indian epics, which usually began, ended, or somehow wound through the ancient mountain range. I had often envisioned myself as one of the protagonists fighting in those timeless stories of good versus evil.

My wife was quiet for a few minutes. I could tell her brain was busy processing the risk factor for such an adventure.

"Well, you have been working nonstop. And you could use a chance to get your stuff together," she teased, wiggling her fingers at my head. "If you really want to go, you should do it."

Chapter 2

"I don't see any record of your booking, sir," said the agent at the Tampa International Airport check-in counter. She smiled politely.

I blinked in disbelief and carefully reviewed the detailed printout of my reservation. My plane was scheduled to leave in two hours.

"But I have a copy of my reservation right here," I insisted. "I booked the ticket months ago." I waved the paper helplessly in front of me.

She looked again at the computer screen, her perfectly manicured fingernails clicking rapidly on the keyboard. She shook her head.

"I'm sorry. What matters is what I see on my screen, and I'm telling you, I have no record of your booking."

Panic hit me in a cold wave. Every subsequent leg of the trip was dependent on landing in Atlanta on time. My journey might be over before it even began. I had to find a way to get on the flight.

"Is there anyone else I can talk to about this? It has to be a mistake."

"I'm sorry. There's nothing more I can do unless you want to book tickets for another time." I could hear an edge creeping into her voice. She stared at me expectantly, her smile losing its enthusiasm as she awaited my answer. She obviously wasn't going to be much help. I turned and walked away.

Potential solutions raced through my mind, all of which seemed improbable. The plane was taking off in less than two hours. In a last-ditch effort to salvage my plans, I called the airline's customer service department. The familiar sound of the company's hold music looped endlessly. I checked my watch. Although it was well after lunchtime, I pictured an entire office of customer service agents slowly chewing sandwiches and sharing stories about all the cute things their pets did. A woman finally answered and assured me she would look into the problem. Then she put me on hold. I was running out of time.

"Sir," she said when she eventually clicked back on the line. "We have a strange situation. I only see your booking from Paris to India. The other flights are full and don't have you listed anywhere as a passenger. I can't get you to Atlanta today."

"What about a flight to New York instead, and then on to Paris?"

"I can get you to New York JFK Airport on a flight that leaves in forty-five minutes, but I don't have the authority to block an international seat to Paris. You would have to take your chances with booking that flight once you land in New York."

It was that or nothing. I accepted my odds and raced to the tram that took me to security. My stomach knotted when I saw the security line snaking through every single turn of the black stanchions, yet I managed to fumble my way through that evil serpent with a handful of minutes to spare. My arms full, carry-on unzipped, boarding pass dangling from my lips, and one shoe threatening mutiny, I stepped onto the plane as they were preparing to close the main door. Everyone inside was staring at me as if I were the reason the plane was still sitting on the ground. Smiling innocently, I tried not to knock seated passengers on the head with the chaos unravelling in my arms. I made my way down the aisle and thankfully squeezed into the last available middle seat. The reassuring click of the seatbelt secured my peace of mind. Perhaps things would go more smoothly from that point on.

Safely on the plane, I closed my eyes and allowed my mind to wander. I imagined sweet monks greeting me at the ashram with glowing faces and deep bows. I envisioned myself meditating in solitude atop the most magnificent mountain range in the world, experiencing the sweet nectarine flow of bliss, all in harmony with the joyous songs of nature.

In reality, I knew very little about where I was headed. I'd fought the instinct to gather too many details about the ashram and its meditation program. I wanted everything to be as unexpected as possible—a true journey of the unknown. For too long, I'd felt my world of habit and familiarity were making my mind dull. Sedate. I also decided not to tell anyone, other than my family, where I was going. I didn't want anyone to muddy my mind with their preconceived notions or biased opinions regarding my unique destination.

When I told my little girl I was leaving on a trip to a faraway mountain, she asked why.

"I've been working too much," I explained to her. "I'm very tired. It would make me feel really good to go somewhere I can relax and not have to worry about anything at all. I can clear my mind to make room for happy things."

"Can't you clean your room for happy things here? And maybe Mommy can make you pan-a-cakes when you're done," she said.

My heart swelled at her take on my problem, the simple profoundness of our exchange quite apparent. I knew I shouldn't have to travel halfway around the world in order to find happiness, but at that point, I didn't know what else to do. My emotions had been teetering like a seesaw for months, constantly tipping back and forth between positivity and negativity. My mood fully depended on which end dropped at any given moment, and it seemed like the weight on the negative side was steadily getting heavier. The truth was, I couldn't stop it on my own. I needed someone to show me how.

I set two goals for myself upon signing up for the trip. My immediate goal was obvious: I wanted to completely unplug myself from all of the electronic input that surrounded me day and night. That would be easy enough at the retreat, I figured, since the nearest cell tower was at least fifty miles away. The long-term goal, floating somewhere near the outskirts of my mind, was more abstract. What did I truly want from the experience? As the plane soared single-mindedly over the endless concerns of the ground, I examined the clouds layered like soft cotton below us. I considered how those unique collections of water vapor exist in a constant state of change. One minute they are light and floating high, only to be dragged down without warning, infused with darkness, and filled with enough sorrow to rain all day. Perhaps my long-term goal should focus on how to convert the transient clouds of peace and happiness in my life into the immovable strength of a mountain.

Chapter 3

As the plane began its descent into New York City, I recalled the first time I landed on American soil at JFK in October of 1996. I had recently graduated at the top of my class from Mysore Medical College and subsequently received several invitations to interview with residency programs around the US. I still remember how I felt making my way out of the international terminal that day. The fall air was crisp and cold, quite unlike what I was used to in India. My mind was steeped in determination, hope, and ambition. I thought of my grandfather, silently thanking him for his guidance throughout my life. If everything went as planned, the beautiful country would become my homeland.

I took the subway to my first interview. Remembering my uncle had warned me about the pickpockets in busy transit systems, I chose to seat myself at the empty end of a subway car. As I enjoyed my space, two men sat down directly on either side of me. Dressed in matching trench coats, their hats pulled low, I found myself—in a moment of complete naiveté—wondering what they were doing. Before I had time to really think about it, one of them jabbed me in the ribs with something black and metallic.

"Give me your money," he said, his voice calm.

"Take whatever you want," I replied, eyes wide.

One of the men grabbed my shiny leather briefcase and threw it aside. The other took my watch. I handed over my wallet, which was deceptively thick with restaurant receipts, ticket stubs, and Indian rupees.

"We're getting off at the next stop. Don't move."

Sure enough, the train stopped, and they got off. Just like that, it was over. Yet, that traumatic moment has survived vividly in my mind ever since. Thankfully, all of my American money and important documents were safe in the briefcase they'd chosen to leave behind.

I must've looked pretty shaken because a woman wearing worn, rumpled clothing approached me and asked if I was okay.

"Those men targeted you because you're dressed so well. Why are you wearing such a nice suit in this part of town?" The concern in her voice was apparent.

"I'm on my way to a job interview," I replied.

"Oh, I see," she said as she realised I was a foreigner. "You know, I'm actually an office professional. I dress like this on the subway to fool people into thinking I have nothing of value. I carry my nice dress clothes in a bag to work every day. Let's get you off the train at the next stop so you can talk to the police."

I exited the train with the woman, and we were able to find a police officer nearby. He asked me what the men had stolen and what they'd pushed against my side to get me to cooperate. I didn't know what it was. I'd never seen anything like it, so I drew a picture of it and described the metal tube on the end.

"Oh, yeah!" the officer exclaimed. "That's definitely an Uzi."

The police officer was kind enough to give me a ride to my interview since it 'wouldn't be safe to walk'.

Somehow, I arrived on time. My nerves were still very much on edge, but I tried to act as if nothing were out of the ordinary and listened to the medical director describe the residency program in detail. At the end of the interview, knowing I wasn't familiar with the city, he began to talk about how safe and family-oriented the surrounding area was.

"Really?" I asked. "Because I got mugged on the way here."

He was shocked. He kept apologising profusely as if it were his fault. "Did they hurt you? Did they take your wallet?"

"They didn't hurt me, but they did take my wallet," I replied.

Frazzled, he handed me a twenty-dollar bill. "Take this so you can catch a cab back to your hotel."

I didn't bother telling him I also felt uneasy taking a cab, but before returning to my hotel, I took off my suit jacket and tie and stuffed them in my briefcase. I also untucked my shirt, ruffled my hair, and wrapped the briefcase in newspaper. The attempt to make myself look completely unappealing to criminals succeeded in getting me safely back to my hotel. Terrified by my interaction with a semi-automatic weapon, I ultimately decided to cancel my remaining job interviews in New York City; I didn't know anyone there, I had no idea which areas were considered safe, and thinking about how to navigate such a large foreign city made me queasy. I ended up buying an unlimited Amtrak pass and spent the next three months in a train car eating peanut butter and jelly sandwiches while crisscrossing the country for job interviews.

Jarred from my thoughts as the wheels of the plane touched down, I glanced at my watch. I needed to find flight options from New York that would get me to Paris on time. I still couldn't believe the leg from Paris to Delhi was the only surviving part of my reservation. Nothing could prepare me for how to negotiate the next two hours, but I knew every minute would count. During the short time it took to deplane, I studied a map of the airport, trying to plan the fastest route to the international terminal.

Once I stepped off the plane, I tried to jog through the terminal, but it was congested with a throng of people moving with all the gusto of a herd of tortoises. I tried to pacify my impatience with a reminder that the uncertainty of my circumstances was liberating in its own way. After all, had I not been looking forward to the element of surprise on my journey? Isn't part of spiritual growth learning to accept things as they are? That all made sense in my mind, but I still felt the stress working its way through my body. I suddenly felt alone and wished my wife were there to help diffuse the tension building within me. She loved to travel, and she'd come with me to visit India soon after we married in the US. Things changed dramatically once we started a family, however. The thought of taking small children on a twenty-hour transatlantic flight—only to face jet lag on the other end—was enough to keep her home.

Eventually, I made it through the crowd and out to the curb. I could still make a flight, but I'd have to hurry. I decided to run along the access road to the international terminal instead of taking the airport train. When I entered the cavernous check-in hall, anxiety hit me like a wall. It was the start of summer break. Countless leisure travellers stood in seemingly endless, winding lines. I had no idea how long it would take me to get a flight to Paris. I quickly considered my ticketing options, scanning the different airline names above each counter. I placed my bet on the one with the fewest people in line.

"Yes, we have five open seats on the next outgoing flight," said the ticket agent. "But all of them are middle seats. We do have another flight later in the evening with aisle seats available, but it looks like that will jeopardise your onward connection."

Even though I'd ended up feeling moderately claustrophobic on the last flight, I was in no position to be picky. There was simply no option to postpone my departure. I had no experience traveling deep into the Himalayas, and my best hope of arriving successfully at the ashram depended on reporting to the rendezvous hotel in Delhi on time.

"Please, give me any seat on the next possible flight."

When I stepped into the behemoth, double-aisled Boeing 747, I paused to take in the plane's magnificence. What a true workhorse, a jewel of the skies, vital to the transatlantic air commute. The gracefulness with which the two-hundred-ton machine can lift itself off the ground is nothing short of astounding. Someone grumbled behind me. My intense admiration for the aircraft was holding up the boarding process. I turned and apologised with an Indian head bobble, then continued down the aisle to my row. There I found my loyal travel companion—the middle seat.

My six-foot-four frame folded reluctantly into the compact space that would be mine for the next eight hours. The average height for a male in my country of birth is five feet, four inches. I made a guess as to how long it would be before my legs started cramping. My wife once joked I'm the tallest man India ever made because at birth, I demanded everything about me be above average. She knows me well. I constantly challenge myself in every aspect of life, always pushing myself to perfectly master any task or challenge presented to me. My wife calls it compulsion. I call it enthusiasm.

I'd even approached my various spiritual practices over the years with the same zealous attitude. In an effort to tame the battle of extremes in my mind, I was constantly investigating different methods to generate quietude and contentment. I jumped from guru to swami to teacher and back again. Even after studying various spiritual paths and meditative techniques, the result was always the same—I was still out of balance. One thing had become certain from my constant exploration: the inherent nature of the human mind is to repel the mundane and displeasing while gravitating towards a multitude of pleasant inputs. I'd spent a good part of my life on a quest to find inner peace, but I realised the search itself was simply another way of indulging my mind's cravings. A deeper part of me aspired to find freedom from the relentless searching altogether.

I envy my wife. She's always been quite capable of moderation and contentment and is rarely restless. She's only ever been devoted to one teacher, the precious Vietnamese Buddhist monk, Thich Nhat Hanh. He stresses the importance of mindfulness, claiming virtually any activity can become a type of meditation if one remains truly present in each moment. Focusing on breath and movement while walking, gardening, or watching children take delight in simple pleasures can all be forms of meditation. I find it extremely difficult to engage in this type of practice, yet I know mastering it would be beneficial. Hahn proposes even mundane chores like washing dishes and mopping the floor can lead to inner peace and profound insight. I'll have to take his word for it, but my wife has certainly found it to be true. Although she'll readily admit, her preferred meditation comes through music.

"The more layers of sound, the better!" she exclaimed one night, her voice rising over the Bose speaker while dancing around the kitchen, cooking dinner. She was listening to 'The Distance to Here by Līve', one of her favourite albums. "I can feel every note in my body, and when I close my eyes, I see the motion of the music in waves of colour." She gestured wildly with her spatula for added emphasis, breathless with glee. To be honest, I'm not entirely convinced what she was doing counts as meditation, but it was really blissing her out, so I kept my mouth shut.

I smiled as I thought of her sweetness. Upon saying goodbye to her and the kids mere hours before, I'd set a resolution for myself. I promised I'd be open to learning whatever spiritual lessons I could from each moment of my journey. I felt like I had already failed my first test by letting the uncertainty of my travel situation get the best of me. Regardless, my hopes were high for the next two weeks. Perhaps sitting in a sacred space with no distractions would allow me to finally uncover a secret, sacred space within my own mind—a place to calm the turmoil of my thoughts once and for all. I'd spent years listening to the wisdom of sages— learning postures, prayers, and rituals. Would the trip finally be what I needed to quell my unrest?

Charles de Gaulle Airport in Paris is virtually a city unto itself and has perfected the art of efficiently moving thousands of people through its borders every day. I spent my long layover observing the differences and similarities among the airport's intriguing cross-section of the human population. Everyone is a stranger until, potentially, they're not. I met the nice German man sitting next to me when I pulled an advanced Mr Bean manoeuvre and spilled some chocolate-covered peanuts on the floor. He watched in amusement as they bounced and scattered, coming to a stop around his feet and under his chair.

"I'm sorry. You're not allergic to nuts, are you?" Reaching around his shoes to retrieve my treats, I grabbed at one, which shot back farther under his seat. I debated for a second whether I should go after it. My wife started calling me Dr Bean for that very reason. Embarrassing mishaps were not uncommon for me. I pictured myself getting stuck under the German man's chair while trying to retrieve the wayward nut, so I decided to leave it there. To my relief, boarding for India began soon after that incident. I bid my new friend *auf Wiedersehen*, hoping never to see him again.

The final flight to India was a breeze. I drifted to sleep in my middle seat somewhere over Central Asia and woke again as the plane was on its final descent into Delhi. An impressive sea of lights greeted me from all directions.

Chapter 4

The time difference between Tampa and Delhi is about eleven hours. My mind was trying to reconcile the darkness outside the airplane window with my body's desire to eat lunch, while my fellow passengers were anxious to disembark so they could go their separate ways. How ironic that the few minutes it takes to deplane can be a greater lesson in patience than the entire nine-hour flight.

That was my first trip to Delhi. I'd grown up thirteen hundred miles to the south, and until then, had no compelling reason to visit. I retrieved the ashram's page of travel instructions from my rucksack. The name and address of the rendezvous hotel were printed in bold across the top. It was located in Paharganj, an area popular with backpackers and low-budget travellers. I was relieved to discover its proximity to the main train station since our train would be leaving in six hours.

The airport's main arrivals area swallowed me into an ocean of humanity. Thousands of faces bobbed up and down, each connected to a body moving in its own direction. Everyone in physical proximity, yet mentally worlds apart. Families crammed against barricades, waiting for the incoming waves to spit out their loved ones. Numerous drivers dotted the scene with placards advertising the names of their charges. In that moment, I was filled with a surge of true anonymity.

I paused at the exit doors to make sure I had everything. As soon as I set foot outside, there would be no way to get back in. Security had been extremely tight in Indian airports since the 2001 terror attack on the Indian Parliament in New Delhi.

Satisfied I hadn't left anything behind, I stepped out into the night air. It was thick with humidity and the smell of vehicle exhaust. Men in khaki pants and shirts immediately surrounded me. Taxi drivers. All of them spoke at once, vying for my business. The prices they offered seemed to depend on the quality of their vehicle. I was too tired to debate options. Speaking in broken Hindi, I chose an offer in the mid-price range.

Hindi is the official language of northern and central India, but where I grew up in the south, Tamil and Kannada are the most commonly spoken languages. Although I learned Hindi as my fourth language in school and can understand it quite well, I felt forbidden to speak it outside of an educational environment. It wasn't an official rule, but more so a product of simmering tensions between those who claimed allegiance to the northern part of the country and the diehard southern nativists. The latter demanded Hindi not be spoken on the streets and would often stop people at random to inquire about their mother tongue. There were many reports of people being assaulted for speaking languages from the north. I was in the seventh grade at that time and remember feeling scared someone would confront me on one of my long walks to school. Luckily, the tension between the two groups eventually faded, but my reluctance to speak Hindi remained.

My driver led me to his car. It was a Maruti—the result of a joint venture between the Indian government and Japan's Suzuki Motor Corporation. Compared to an American sedan, it was tiny. The windows were rolled down halfway, and I couldn't tell which was louder—the driver trying to shout over the din of the airport traffic or the mechanical buzz coming from the engine. Although it wasn't the time or place I wanted to have a conversation, I tested my language skills, hoping to gain insight about the hotel from a local.

It was well after midnight by then. We turned off the broad four-lane highway and entered the heart of the city. Narrow side alleys crisscrossed each other in no particular pattern. We drove past shuttered storefronts, the streets mostly deserted. I only saw occasional groups of people. They were huddled over open pushcarts with gas lanterns and large cooking vessels with rising steam. It felt strange to be awake while the city slept. Even the air was still as if in a state of rest.

Streetlights cast long shadows on the ground as the car turned one way, then another. It felt like we were going in circles. Everything looked the same to me. Fear crept into my mind, convincing me I was being led away to some hidden corner of the city where I'd be waylaid and robbed. After all, it made sense. I was in a new place, and the driver was a complete stranger. It was the middle of the night—there would be no one around to help. As my body geared up to launch its adrenaline, we turned onto a narrow street with a few open storefronts and some foot traffic. I felt slightly better and forced my mind to settle, reminding myself the man was a professional who'd likely driven hundreds of people before me.

The pocket-sized convenience stores were selling essentials for late-night ramblers. My gaze moved from the cigarettes to the bottled water before settling on the homemade fried snacks packaged in day-old newspaper. I wondered when I would get to eat next. Rolls of shiny plastic pouches with bright colouring hung like confetti behind the store owners. They were packages of *gutka*—a mixture of chewing tobacco, crushed betel nut, and spices.

The car finally pulled to a stop in front of a three-story building that looked like it housed apartments. Several steep, narrow, marble steps led up to the double glass doors. After forty-five minutes of driving, I'd made it to the hotel safely. I thanked the driver profusely and gave him a generous tip. Exhaustion overtook me as I trudged up the stairs.

The front desk attendant was also the manager on duty. When he saw me, he broke into a broad grin, revealing his gutka-stained teeth and bright lips. I placed my rucksack on a cloth couch in the reception area as he greeted me with delight.

"Welcome to India, sir! Are you with the meditation group? Almost everyone has checked in. I have a room on the top floor for you. Simply leave your passport with me, and I will give you the key." He held out his hand.

I froze.

His head bobbed in reassurance.

I wasn't about to part with such an important document. It was one of my most valued possessions. As soon as I became an American citizen and got my United States passport, I made an excessive number of photocopies. I stuffed them in various safe spots around the house and in my office. One day my wife called and said, "I was cleaning the kids' room, and I found a stack of passport copies in one of their little desk drawers. Should I leave it there, or what?"

"Yes, please. Leave it there. I consider that a strategic location."

"I wonder if you were a squirrel in your previous life," she pondered. "Really. That would explain so much."

"It's just in case," I told her. "You know, in case the original gets stolen; in case no one believes I'm an American; in case I fall and hit my head and lose my memory along with the original document…"

"Sir?" the front desk manager inquired.

"Sorry. Uh, I have a copy I can leave with you. I hope that will suffice," I replied.

He squinted at the copy, then the original, moving his head back and forth several times until he was satisfied. He scribbled something illegible on a piece of paper and handed my passport back. I grabbed the room key, looking forward to some real sleep.

When I opened the door to my room, I was immediately greeted by a blast of hot, musty air. The ceiling fan wobbled at full speed, making a loud whirring sound. Thick, dark curtains danced against the wall as stale air whipped up from behind them. The bed was a bowed twin mattress on a simple wood frame that was a few inches too short for me. A small side table with a cup and thermos were the only other accessories in the room.

The stifling air was making me extremely uncomfortable, and I wasn't sure what to do. I could go with the flow and accept the situation, or I could ask for another room. Before I decided, an ancient window-mounted air conditioning unit caught my eye. Problem solved. I'd turn it on, and the room could cool off while I showered. I plugged it into the exposed wall socket. The fan inside made a horrendous high-pitched noise before falling silent, then the wiring started to spark and sputter. The sparking continued on and off every few seconds. My reaction time was severely delayed by fatigue, but I managed to yank the power cord out of the wall before the curtains caught fire. The cord ejected from the socket along with a generous piece of plaster from the wall. *Oops.* My wife's voice tumbled through my head. "Dr Bean. Paging Dr Bean."

I reported to the front desk and requested a different room. When I finally collapsed on the mattress in my new room, the bed frame groaned and made several cracking noises. I braced myself for impact, but she held steady. A broken air conditioner was plenty; I didn't want to have to explain a shattered cot.

For all the physical discomfort that comes with jet lag, there's definitely a positive. When sleep does come, it's deep and dreamless. The notion of time disappears completely. Waking up from such an experience is truly rejuvenating.

I closed my eyes. Loud clanging sounds came from outside the window, accompanied by occasional yelling. I dozed off and on for a couple of hours, trying to ignore the noise. It persisted. I peered out the window to see a group of teenagers running around with sticks, playing their version of street hockey. Men huddled around a gas stove with a steaming pot, perhaps brewing their early-morning chai. Streetlights lining the road were in a constant state of flickering, undecided on whether to brighten the street or plunge it into darkness. Narrow shop fronts advertised everything from food to used auto parts. Migrant workers lay on the pavement, their only option for a night's rest. Their situation made mine look like a five-star experience. I prayed for their well-being.

Although I was drowsy, I didn't want to risk going back to bed. I was afraid I would oversleep and miss my ride into the mountains. I splashed water on my face and sat in a cross-legged posture, my back perfectly straight. Anyone watching me would surely think I'd mastered the art of meditation, but they'd never see the endless parade of thoughts marching through my mind.

I was impatient to get to the ashram. I imagined sitting in the cool reaches of the Himalayan foothills. That single thought blossomed into a full-blown scene replete with birds chirping and leaves rustling in the summer breeze. I could practically hear the gurgle of a nameless rivulet waiting to join the mighty Ganges, taking a scenic trip through the great northern plains of India and finally emptying into the Bay of Bengal. The effortless flow of water was such an appealing escape in that moment, I wondered if I'd be allowed to sit in silence next to the river near the ashram.

With departure time approaching, I made a video call to my wife back in the States. I knew it would be the last time I spoke with her for at least two weeks. I told her about my travel adventures thus far and said hi to the kids. She encouraged me to adopt any homeless street children I encountered along the way. We continued to speak for quite a while, but as soon as I hung up, it felt like our conversation had lasted an instant.

Feeling reenergised, I took a cold shower and rearranged my rucksack. I put my money and essentials—like my passport—right in the middle, then everything else in concentric circles. Perhaps that would keep my valuables safe from pickpockets. There would be plenty of people—even kids—trying to make a living as petty thieves at New Delhi Central. I immediately felt compassion for them, understanding their desperate situation. No one should have to live that kind of life. Children, especially, don't belong on pavements and railway stations—they belong in safe homes and schools. I took out several hundred-rupee notes, roughly a dollar each. I might not be able to adopt any children, but I could certainly buy them a substantial meal.

Chapter 5

A rooster crowed from the alley outside my window. It was time to meet my fellow seekers. Nervous anticipation grew in my mind. Questions arose in rapid-fire succession. *Who are the other people on this trip? Will the drive up the mountainside be safe? Am I going to be able to maintain complete silence for the entire retreat?* And, most importantly, *When on earth are we going to eat?*

The modest lobby area was packed with milling bodies. Since official silence wouldn't begin until we set foot in the ashram, unfamiliar faces greeted each other with plentiful chatter. Several languages rose over the hum of conversation, including French, Spanish, Hindi, and English. All of the competing noise made me want to get a head start on the silence. I had no wish to engage in pleasantries. There was already a roaring discussion going on in my mind—no need to add to the cacophony.

The group piled their collective luggage against the wall. Numerous suitcases, bags, and backpacks were stacked in a mound stretching to the ceiling, but I kept my rucksack safely pinned to my back. I didn't want to encourage an avalanche. Although I was traveling light, especially compared to some of the jumbo suitcases at the base of the heap, I had no doubt I was carrying as much mental baggage as anyone else. After the retreat, I hoped to return to that lobby lighter in both mind and spirit.

At 6:00 a.m., a young Indian man squeezed his way into the middle of the crowd and raised his hands to quiet everyone. He wore a pure white cotton dhoti that looked like a cross between a sarong and trousers. Marks of sacred ash were smeared across his forehead. He introduced himself as a Brahmachari Jeevan, apprentice monk in-training. A few moments later, Guru Ananda—the senior monk and leader of the retreat—joined him. Ananda was dressed in traditional ochre monastic apparel. He had a balding head and a bright smile. A bushy, salt-and-pepper beard framed his round, cherubic face, highlighting an air of childlike innocence about him. His eyes exuded sincerity and compassion. It was a joy to finally be face-to-face with the person who would guide my spiritual course for the next fifteen days.

A second apprentice monk and three volunteers accompanied Guru Ananda and outlined the instructions for the day's travel. We would be allowed to talk, but we couldn't wander off from the group at any time. There would be a head count every step of the way. From the time we left the hotel to the time we got off the train in Haridwar, each of us was responsible for keeping track of our own belongings. I was dismayed to realise, upon the end of the briefing, there had been no mention of breakfast. My stomach was lodging audible complaints at that point. As far as my internal clock was concerned, I was approaching dinnertime and had skipped breakfast and lunch.

I already knew food wasn't necessarily high on the list of priorities for those on the monastic path. I'd heard stories of student monks who were forbidden to eat until their teacher ate, and they were allowed one meal a day. I also knew there were certain days each month set aside for fasting, usually coinciding with the lunar cycle. I tried to remember if the lunar calendar was mentioned anywhere in the retreat's description. With much relief, I recalled the program guide indicated each day would be organised around meals (plural), individual and group meditations, free time, study, and rest. My relief was short lived, however, when I remembered something else. One of our meditation guidelines was not to practice on a full stomach. It could make the mind sluggish. What if we were given sparse meals? Was I going to be expected to use hunger as a tool for developing patience and tolerance in uncomfortable situations? I truly hoped not. I prayed the meal portions would be generous.

There were about forty of us in the group, and we made a beeline to the buses waiting outside. We were asked to watch our bags as they were loaded before continuing on board. I offered my assistance to the scrawniest porter since he had the task of loading almost one hundred bags into the luggage compartment. As I was wedging a suitcase into place, the exhaust pipe expelled a black cloud of acrid diesel exhaust in my direction. I coughed and sputtered. Wiping the soot from my face, I imagined I must look like a cartoon character. I became even more impatient for the fresh air of the Himalayas.

Once we boarded the bus and were duly counted, our journey as a group began. People wasted little time delving into conversation. Bonds of friendships were already beginning to forge. I resisted my weak impulse to communicate with anyone, pretending to be lost in my own open-eyed meditation. My vacant look projected the message,

There were six seats in each row, divided by a narrow aisle running down the middle of the train. Metal grilles barred the windows from the outside, presumably to protect the glass. I located my assigned spot and secured my belongings. Once again reunited with the middle seat, I took my place between two men from my group.

"G'day, mate. How you going?" asked the man to my left. "I'm Tim." I guessed him to be an Aussie, but he said he was from New Zealand.

"Namaste. How are you? I'm Jacques," said the burly man on my right with a thick French accent.

I introduced myself and listened while they conversed. They were in a chirpy mood and talking a mile a minute. I wanted to relax in silence, but to avoid an awkward train ride, there was little choice but to join the conversation. While I commiserated with the others about the ravages of jet lag, it occurred to me how momentous the occasion was. There I was, sandwiched between two people from opposite ends of the world, and we were all headed to the same destination.

At that point, my stomach felt like it was turning inside out, and my sole focus was to pacify my hunger. It took great effort not to display discomfort on my face. I eyed a bag of trail mix on Tim's lap, and my mouth watered at the thought of dried cranberries, crunchy almonds, and bittersweet chunks of dark chocolate. No wonder Tim was so talkative and amiable. He must've already loaded up on the mood-enhancing mix barely out of my reach.

A gangly young man holding an oversized cardboard box came down the aisle, handing out miniature bottled waters that would barely fill half of a coffee mug.

"Will there be breakfast served?" I asked in passable Hindi.

"It is coming, sir. Once the train leaves the station and the tickets are punched by the ticket collector, we will serve hot breakfast."

Those words delighted me, but even though I knew breakfast was coming soon, my mind was begging me to ask Tim for a helping of his trail mix. If that was another test of the trip, I was failing miserably. So much of my mood was reliant on food. A few hours of hunger, and my whole mindset shifted from thoughts of a transcendental achievement to existential dread.

I gulped the water down and politely asked Tim for a handful of his trail mix. He kindly obliged—may he live a long life in peace and harmony. As he jiggled the bag to drop some nuts and chocolates into my open palm, I outstretched the other hand as well, hoping it too would be filled. I admonished myself for being greedy, but holy cow, it was so good. With my stomach somewhat satisfied, I climbed out of my dark hole and settled into a wonderful mood, waxing philosophical with my new travel mates.

Chapter 6

The train lurched forward, causing me to sway in my seat. It felt good to be moving once more, ever closer to the ashram. We began to pick up speed, the railway platform steadily receding into the past. The train heaved itself across a massive bridge stretching over the sandy banks of the Yamuna River. Wide grassy fields greeted us on the other side, serving as a sudden contrast to the narrow streets and gridlocked traffic we'd left behind. As quickly as the green space appeared, it was gone, the landscape continuously transforming. In the distance, tall earth toned buildings stood against the horizon. Rows upon rows of tightly spaced houses flashed below us. I could clearly see their flat rooftops, many of which were speckled with colourful silk clothes drying in the sun. The modest but adequate homes soon gave way to the makeshift metal roofs of thousands of slum dwellings glinting in the sun. Tim and Jacques fell silent as their eyes filled with a reality they'd never before witnessed.

Our view turned tranquil and uplifting once we were beyond the confines of the city. We traversed miles of village farmland casually dotted with thatch-roofed houses. The passenger car gently rocked side to side, lulling me into a sense of calm. The wheels made their predictable *tak, tak, tak* sounds as they encountered the spaces in the track designed to accommodate the expansion and contraction of metal rails. The monotonous vista, along with the repetitive movement and sounds, created a soothing, meditative atmosphere.

I noticed the ticket collector quietly and efficiently clipping tickets, then quickly returning them to waiting hands. At that rate, food service couldn't be far behind. I closed my eyes and tried to imagine what flavours awaited me. As the positive effects from Tim's trail mix were wearing off, our promised hot breakfast arrived. My mind took part in a silent celebration as soon as I discovered they were serving my favourite South Indian meal. Steamed rice and lentil cakes— called *idlis*—served with spicy, soupy vegetable *sambar*. Normally, when I'm famished, my main goal is to transfer food from my mouth to my stomach as quickly as possible. That time, though, I made my best effort to be mindful, savouring every bite. It wasn't a very big serving, and I didn't know when we were scheduled to eat again.

Eventually, curiosity got the better of me, and I asked Jacques why he decided to join the retreat.

"The work has kept me busy for many years, yes?" he replied with his distinct French accent. "Same thing every week. To work, home, to work, home. I am now restless. Ah, unable to concentrate. I hope the retreat can help me to again get the focus."

I suspected there was more Jacques wanted to say but wasn't volunteering.

"What about you, Tim?" I asked.

"Been a librarian all my life, mate. My world's always been about books. I've read heaps of viewpoints that aren't mine. I want to explore my own a bit now, eh? My family, my life, they're good as gold, but something deeper is missing. I met Guru Ananda in Christchurch at a talk last year. I didn't know what to expect, but it was sweet as, Bro. Really something else. He gave us a practice to try. Told us to pay close attention to external reactions and habits instead of going along with them like we normally do. I gave it a go. Sometimes it was a cracker of a day—fun, like a game. Other days were bloody awful, but the process itself was genius. It was a real eye-opener for me. Made me think about how my mind reacts to each moment."

I nodded in understanding—kind of. Tim's Kiwi slang lost me a little.

Jacques had a troubled look on his face. "Are you okay?" I asked.

"I wish everything could be so simple. Ah, to watch this thought. Or that habit," he said. "Honestly, my life—it's in shambles." Jacques lowered his head, his eyes filling with tears. "My wife of twenty years, she leaves me. I come home one day, she is gone. There is a note on the fridge—the number of her divorce lawyer. It took me a week to overcome the shock. I am now divorced. I learned of this trip at the Indian Temple in Montreal, where I enjoy food on Sundays. Whenever I am there, they make me like family. But then I go home to the apartment. It is empty. I am lonely. My wife has taken everything I had, you see? So I am now desperate. I put all of my money into this trip. I hope for a miracle."

He began sobbing. It was quite jarring to see him break down like that when a couple of hours before he appeared so jovial and carefree. I put one arm around his back and offered him a paper napkin I'd saved from the breakfast tray.

"I apologise." He sniffled. "I lost control. I am usually very, ah, strong inside. Thank you for listening. I feel better."

He wiped his eyes and sat up a little straighter, releasing a deep, shaky exhale as if any remaining bits of overwhelming emotion were leaving his body.

I'd been sitting still so long I couldn't ignore the need to stretch my legs any longer. I walked directly to the back of the train car and out the door onto the covered gangway, expecting some fresh countryside air.

It was like I'd been thrust into an entirely different world. My senses were assaulted. Violent shaking replaced the gentle rocking I'd felt inside the cabin as the train cars protested their coupling. The friction of the wheels bearing down on the metal track turned the soothing *tak, tak, tak* sound into a deafening chorus of squeals. I was thrown sideways as the train turned, and I fumbled to grab the railing. I'd learned my lesson; I returned back to the quiet confines of my protective middle seat.

Guru Ananda rose slowly to make an announcement. A hush trickled through the car, even among people not in our group. In India, a person wearing the ocherous clothing of a monastic is revered regardless of their specific spiritual path.

"Namaste, and welcome everyone," he said with a smooth, warm voice. "My spiritual brothers and sisters, I hope this journey we are undertaking together is transformational for you. I have met a few of you during my travels, but every day is a fresh start and a clean slate. Assume you don't know me, and I don't know you. We are here to support each other on a spiritual exploration. This is not a trip for pleasure or relaxation. We are on a mission. There is only one way inward: through the mind. Our goal is to give you all the tools to succeed. Long ago, my master placed his hands on my head and told me he cracked the code to inner peace. He did not tell me there were years, possibly decades or even lifetimes, of practice in front of me to turn that code into something tangible. I, myself, am still a work in progress. But my duty is to share with you whatever I can from my experiences."

Guru Ananda then motioned for Brahmachari Jeevan to take over. With a clipboard, he shuffled row to row, checking names off his list. As he came closer, I could see his features clearly. He was young—I guessed about twenty-five. He had a smooth complexion, high cheekbones, and almond-shaped eyes. His facial features suggested he was from the far eastern part of India. Perhaps from the region of Bengal, famous for its rich cultural history, remarkable saints, and the beautiful Bengal tiger.

Earlier, at the train station in New Delhi, I'd seen the apprentice monks carrying one small backpack each. Their luggage created a stark contrast to the bulky suitcases of our entourage. Monks-in-training don't need much, though. Everything is taken care of, including room, board, and access to all the spiritual treasures of the East. It doesn't necessarily mean their lives are easy; much more is expected of a monk than of regular disciples, such as myself. It would've been virtually impossible for someone like me to become a monk at that point in my life. I had far too many worldly responsibilities: a wife and young children, elderly parents, and a business to run. Others in my group surely had their own strings pulling them away from the monastic path as well. Regardless, I knew the next couple of weeks would offer all of us a taste of life as a renunciant. We'd be able to feel the dedication it took to turn fleeting glimpses of awareness and peace into lasting assets to be called upon at a moment's notice.

Brahmachari Jeevan moved to the front of the car and began to speak. His voice was pleasantly soft, but not everyone could hear him. A microphone and a portable speaker quickly materialised, which, thankfully, didn't seem to bother the other passengers in the car. The train, after all, was heading to one of the holiest cities in India. The travellers likely had their own gurus to visit. A few of them even turned or stood to listen. The young apprentice monk officially held centre stage in the moving train. He closed his eyes and folded his hands in prayer, the microphone between his palms. He opened with a *bhajan*: a song in praise of the divine.

Three gods compose the Hindu trinity—Brahma, Shiva, and Vishnu. They are the creator, destroyer, and sustainer, respectively. Each of them has thousands of corresponding manifestations and incarnations—like Krishna, for example—who are also worshiped. Truly, the Hindu pantheon offers a 'the more, the merrier' approach, which gives devotees great freedom to pray to whomever they choose. Do you need help overcoming one of life's many obstacles? There's a god for that—his name is Ganesha. Money woes? Pray to the goddess Lakshmi; she'll take care of you. Are you trying to muster up some physical or mental strength? Hanuman's your guy. The possibilities are virtually endless.

India's history and culture are deeply interwoven with fascinating accounts of how all those different deities came to be, and around 80 percent of the country's population is Hindu. Despite this, Mother India has plenty of room in her heart for the followers of other religions, such as Jains, Sikhs, Christians, and Muslims. She's also been an unwavering friend to Tibetan Buddhists in exile from China, consistently welcoming them across her borders with open arms.

As Brahmachari Jeevan continued his bhajan, a few hesitant claps around the car began to punctuate the hymn's rhythm. By the time he'd increased the cadence and pitch of his song, everyone was clapping along. At the crescendo, people stood, letting their bodies move with each beat. I glanced over at Jacques; he was sitting with his mouth agape. Both he and Tim seemed to be enjoying the spectacle. The song slowed again and faded out with one last long note. Loud cheers followed the ending, and the young monk grinned sheepishly.

Brahmachari Jeevan continued with a few announcements. We were scheduled to arrive in Haridwar in a little over an hour, at half-past eleven.

"When we get to Haridwar," he said, "please follow Brahmachari Krishna as you alight from the train." He motioned to his brother monk, who was silently seated by the window. Brahmachari Krishna was unassuming, perhaps even a bit bashful. Until that moment, I hadn't seen him make eye contact with anyone. Raising his head, he met the group's gaze. He cracked a smile, folded his hands in the traditional greeting of Namaste, and added a slight head bobble for emphasis.

"It is very important for you to stay together. Haridwar will be an unfamiliar place for you, and we are on a schedule. It takes eight hours to drive up the mountain, and there are forest checkpoints along the way. We must clear them before sunset. If they close, we will be stuck in the forest overnight in our Jeeps. There are also wild animals, such as tigers." His eyes widened, and he paused to let the gravity of his last statement sink in. "We will stop at a tea stall to get drinks and snacks. There will be a washroom as well. But please, this is not a holiday. We will stop for ten minutes."

The monk wrapped up his list of housekeeping items with a quotation from one of Guru Ananda's books, one meant to stoke the smouldering embers of a spiritual quest within the aspirant.

"Happiness becomes permanent if we see everyone as part of ourselves and see ourselves in everyone."

Jacques looked concerned after that last bit.

"I did not think fully about this trip. I felt it was a good idea at the time I said yes, but I do not know anything about the meditation. I feel like I am not going to, ah, understand the meaning of the teachings. I do not even know what is a guru."

Poor Jacques. He simply wanted a cushion on which to rest his weary, post-divorce emotional state. He really did seem unprepared for such a foreign and rigorous routine.

"Don't worry, Jacques," I said. "I'd be happy to explain about gurus."

"That is helpful." Jacques sounded relieved. "Please share what you know."

Tim also showed great interest, so I began.

"The word 'guru' actually means 'dispeller of darkness'. In Buddhism and Hinduism, it's a spiritual guide or teacher— usually a person with the authority to initiate someone into a specific school of belief or path to enlightenment. These days, with the Internet, you can gain access to gurus of all kinds. But in earlier times, they usually lived in forests and remote hermitages. Without roads or addresses, it was nearly impossible to find them. Seekers often endured great

52

difficulties to locate a guru. Because of that, once a seeker was accepted into a hermitage, he usually stayed there for years, or even for life."

"Are there places like that nowadays? Where gurus live and meditate in forests, then?" asked Tim as he leaned in to listen.

"Yes, actually. There's a sect of *sadhus*—Indian holy men—called *Avadhootas*. They're mystics who have no worldly attachments, no true possessions. Occasionally, not even clothes. Some of them have long hair worn in *jata* locks, like dreadlocks, and cover their bodies in ash. It's almost as if they have one foot here on earth and the other in some kind of transcendental realm. They can live anywhere, but they often frequent certain parts of the Himalayas, like where we're going."

"That's mean as! Living out in the wops with nothing," Tim said in awe. "I could never do that."

Jacques agreed. "Amazing. I could not do it, either. I am not good at being by myself. I am afraid with two weeks of quiet, I will be sitting alone too much with my worries."

"Aw, she'll be right, Jacques," Tim said. "I'd bet a hundred dollars every bloke here feels like that. We all have struggles, for sure. As far as I'm concerned, my mind can go one of two ways. It either comes under my control, or I'm under its control. There's no in between for me. I battle my desires with patience, eh. If patience outlasts the desire, it wins. And if desires are strong enough, my patience fails."

Tim intrigued me. His eyes reflected inner calmness, and his speech hinted at a deep understanding.

"Tim, you sound like a guru," I told him.

"Yeah, nah. Not so fast. I don't think I'd be able to wear the clothes. Seem too restrictive." Tim laughed as he tugged on his loose sweatpants.

The train was going at a steady clip. We would reach Haridwar soon. I glanced at the luggage rack overhead to make sure my rucksack was still there. We'd been so engrossed in our discussion that anyone could have easily walked away with my things. Even though I only had one bag, I was definitely no Avadhoota. My rucksack was packed to the zippers with items I deemed necessary for the retreat, like my inflatable meditation cushion. I knew I wouldn't last long sitting on the floor without it. My back was a mess due to years spent wearing a heavy protective lead apron during stenting procedures. Since the real-time X-ray of a patient's body is needed to find blockages and place stents properly, the radiation exposure is much higher than a typical X-ray. I'd been undergoing weekly neuromuscular therapy sessions to get my back into decent working order. I hoped it would behave during the retreat.

I preferred to believe everything I'd stuffed in my rucksack was essential for the journey. I'd begun shopping months before for everything I'd bring with me. Even though there were no hikes planned by the ashram, life was different in my fantasy world. I imagined myself climbing up the side of a steep mountain, seeking a special spot with an inspiring view where I could meditate in complete solitude. Such a feat would require proper equipment, I reasoned. But once I passed the threshold into the outdoor outfitters store filled with so many useful gadgets and survival tools, I knew I was in for a fierce battle between my needs and my desires. It was a glorious place, indeed.

I tried on every kind of camping backpack and chose the one that seemed to speak to me the most. Then I traded it for another one after a round of eeny, meeny, miny, moe. The salesperson ensured the new backpack fit properly by filling it with ten-pound bags of sand layered one on top of another. He measured my torso height and adjusted where the pack sat on my back, cinching down on the load-lifting straps. I walked around the store while my mind carried me to the mountain trails. I imagined resting my head on the pack after a long day of hiking as I pondered the night sky, alive with billions of stars.

Of course, I needed proper hiking shoes as well, but I waited until my second trip to the store to buy those. I even researched headlamps so I could sound knowledgeable about lumens and wattages when I went back to the store for my third round. On my fourth visit, I bought camp mugs and towels. The biodegradable soap was another good buy. Admittedly, I got carried away, but I was able to stop myself while investigating cloth braces for my ankles and knees—I had to draw the line somewhere. There were so many distractions in the store that I almost forgot to purchase a potentially life-saving UV water purifier. I knew I could get all sorts of harmful microbes from river water, but I'd completely forgotten about any possible rainfall, so I never bought a poncho, rain jacket, or umbrella.

I lost count of how many times I went shopping, but every time I returned home, I'd lay my bounty out on the bed, sampling the new items and seeing how they would fit in with everything else I'd already bought.

At one point, after returning the backpack I'd already been fitted for, I brought home three others. I filled each one to see which was most comfortable to carry. I wasn't paying any attention to how often I ended up exchanging a purchase for something slightly different only to decide, in the end, I didn't really need it at all. I suspected my wife was becoming exasperated with my indecisiveness due to the increasing altitude of her right eyebrow, but for the longest time, she never said anything. She simply observed.

Then, one day, she finally broke her silence.

Sitting precariously on the edge of the bed in the one remaining space unoccupied by my purchases, she said, "This is really painful to watch. Pick a bag, pack the most important items, and be done with it. Why are you spending so much time and energy picking out stuff? Isn't half the point of this retreat to reduce distractions from material items so you can focus on spiritual growth? Why are you doing this?"

"Uh… because I only recently realised how much I like to shop?" I hoped it was a valid reason.

"Oh, for crying out loud." She threw her hands in the air.

She had a valid point, so I conceded and told her I obviously needed the experience in order to match her level of wisdom. She merely laughed and rolled her eyes.

On the train, I was missing my wife's company but enjoying the time with my new travel companions. Something had caught Tim's attention, and he was staring out the window. We were very close to the train station in Haridwar. All I could see were the illegal makeshift tenements on either side of the tracks, similar to what we'd seen in the poorest areas of New Delhi.

"I can't believe it! Look! A fully grown adult is mooning the train!" he exclaimed.

I had to break the news to Tim. The unfortunate reality about India is that people living in the slums don't have indoor plumbing or otherwise appropriate places to answer the call of nature. Each successive government pledges to end the practice of open defecation, but getting a roof over everyone's head is challenging enough. Jacques and Tim were equally aghast at the rapid immersion into another country's impoverished subculture.

Our conversation ended as the train slowed and approached the station in Haridwar. There was no guarantee we would sit together on the drive up the mountain, and we would be entering silence as soon as we arrived at the ashram. Our eyes said it all as we looked at each other and smiled. I was grateful for having such wonderful seatmates. They'd made the five-hour trip a true pleasure.

Jacques seemed a little uneasy that we were parting ways, but Tim reassured him he would watch out for him. They'd formed a bond, and I sensed Jacques was going to lean on Tim for support for the duration of the trip. I also offered to be of assistance although I knew it would be challenging while adhering to a strict code of silence.

Chapter 7

The train released a final shudder as it came to a complete stop in Haridwar, casting off any remnants of momentum it had gathered during the previous five hours. Even though we were no longer moving, I could still feel a gentle rocking in my body. A few of us—including me—stood quickly, anxious to leave. Brahmachari Jeevan shot out of his seat like a rocket, frantically waving for us to sit back down. Despite the noise outside, we could hear his animated voice clearly without the microphone.

"Please stay seated! We need a head count!"

At first, I thought that seemed unnecessary. After all, the express train had never stopped. How could anyone be missing? Then my mind replayed the scene from my moments on the gangway, how I'd been thrown into the railing. Suppose I'd been thrown over the edge and been stranded somewhere along the tracks, waiting for someone to realise what happened to me? I decided to never again question the compulsory count.

Once the monk was satisfied with the number of heads present, we were allowed to disembark. Two porters collected all the luggage and deposited it on the platform, but I insisted on carrying my rucksack. After all, I'd spent hours picking it out and getting properly fitted for it. We'd developed a bond, and I was reluctant to part with it.

Thousands of people were crowded in and around the train station, and even though we were on the threshold of a much higher elevation, it was just plain hot. Somehow, not too far from the main entrance, we managed to find a relatively calm and quiet spot under an enormous tree. The entire lot of us gratefully took refuge in her shade. I longed to move and stretch my body, and the temptation to wander around gnawed at me. However, the last thing I wanted was to cause trouble. I reluctantly stayed with the others while awaiting further instructions. Brahmachari Jeevan had darted off to see about the food, and Guru Ananda was nowhere in sight; we were told he'd gone to meet his local contact for the Jeeps.

When the lunch packets arrived, our group broke apart into several smaller clusters to sit on the ground and eat. Chattering and laughter would occasionally rise from one group or another into the branches of our tree. From where I was sitting, I could see everything happening around the train station. I noticed several homeless beggars—a heart-breaking sight made worse when my eyes came to rest upon a young man with no legs. He was dragging his body along the ground, the bottom of his torso protected by a burlap bag. It was folded over on itself several times to provide meagre cushioning. I looked down at my expensive hiking boots and suddenly felt horrible. I'd made sure to break them in before the adventure lest I suffer a blister. The man didn't even have stumps to be fitted with prostheses, yet he held a smile on his face as he tirelessly inquired among travellers in the dusty parking lot. If he didn't receive anything, no ill will or disappointment registered on his face. He simply carried his unwavering smile with him to the next group. I was enjoying the shade while he was diligently working in the heat.

I hadn't started eating yet. I gave him my lunch.

The ancient Indian caste system was very much alive within the masses of people in motion around us. For centuries, the caste hierarchy has divided Indian society into four main groups: priests (Brahmins), warriors (Kshatriyas), farmers/traders (Vaishyas), and servants/laborers (Shudras). The system began as a way to classify the type of job a person held, but eventually, it became tied to genetic lines. Therefore, a person is confined to the caste into which they're born. It's impossible to move from one group to another. This system has historically been used as an excuse to discriminate against individuals in so-called lower castes—especially those belonging to a fifth group: the Scheduled Caste, also referred to as Dalits or Untouchables. In modern-day India, it's illegal to discriminate against people because of their caste. This has led to an increase in the ability for lower castes to seek higher education and non-traditional careers. Yet, far too many people still believe that when Dalits partake in 'unclean' work, such as trash picking and cleaning latrines, it makes them impure and inherently less worthy. I wondered how many of the beggars in the parking lot were Dalit, unable to get a suitable job due to their caste status.

Brahmins were overrepresented in the crowd, but I wasn't surprised. Haridwar is considered a holy city due to both its historical significance and proximity to the Ganges River. Easily distinguished by their appearance, the priests sported shaved heads with a tuft of hair remaining at the back. Their foreheads were each marked with a colourful *tilak*, indicating their sectarian affiliation. Most of them wore the same type of dhoti as our monks.

Haridwar is also a popular destination during the summer, so the traders were bustling about, hoping to sell their goods. A few ambitious merchants had established their presence in stalls across the busy main street. The others, without a fixed roof under which to operate, were mobile and resourceful. Nimble-footed and holding overflowing baskets full of souvenirs, trinkets, and toys, they steered their way through throngs of potential customers. Every hour, new trains unloaded and took aboard new passengers. It didn't matter to the traders which way someone was headed, only that they had money to spend.

Our group, full of tourists, initially attracted generous attention. Every vendor in sight approached us, but we had our game faces on. There were more serious things on our minds than cheap trinkets. We were after the ultimate prize: moving up a notch or two on the spiritual ladder. Once they realised we had no interest in their material goods, they wasted no time scattering in all different directions.

Brahmachari Jeevan had kept busy since getting off the train. Flitting to and fro, he'd constantly been taking care of various tasks.

"I hope you did not overload your stomachs," he said to us as he passed by. "There will be lots of winding road for the next several hours."

His words repeated in my mind, and I suddenly felt cemented to my spot under the tree. Back when my wife suggested I find a retreat centre in the US, one of her concerns about the Himalayas stemmed from my propensity for severe motion sickness.

"Do you really want to spend hours driving up the side of a mountain? Remember what happened in Hawaii?" she asked.

I'd surprised my bride with a honeymoon vacation to Maui. One morning, we decided to take a popular day trip called the Road to Hana—a drive covering over sixty miles of coastal highway zigging and zagging its way around the edge of the island. The road is full of narrow spots, hairpin turns, and rising elevation. The reward for the agonising ride, though, is to experience some of the most breath-taking views on the planet. Unfortunately, we'd only conquered about five of the switchbacks before we started feeling queasy. My wife was mildly uncomfortable at that point, but I felt so sick I had to pull over.

"Can you look at the guidebook and see how many more turns there are before the end?" I asked, thinking we could try and tough it out.

"Okay, yeah. Uh, it says here..." She trailed off, then laughed incredulously before finishing. "Six hundred. There's no way we are going to make it. Even if we get there, we'd have to repeat everything on the way back. So make that twelve hundred."

It was settled. I made a U-turn, and we warily navigated the twisted road back to sea level.

Of course I'd remembered that event, but I'd opted to ignore it in my excitement for the Himalayas. With the mountainous drive so close at hand, though, the reality of my situation was suddenly terrifying. As the thought of eight hours intensified with turn after turn after turn, a prickling fear spread throughout my body. Why had I chosen to ignore the issue earlier, simply noting it as a potentially minor problem?

I'd even dismissed my wife's suggestion to pack some motion sickness medicine. I was filled with regret for not taking her advice seriously. Again. I couldn't count all the times in our marriage she'd offered helpful advice, and I'd chosen to brush it aside without a second thought. I vowed to consider her suggestions more seriously once I got home. After all, she was only trying to look out for me.

By then, Guru Ananda had returned with Brahmachari Krishna and a few locals in tow. They were all disciples of the guru and were there to help us get situated in the Jeeps and to see us off as we headed farther north. They stood close to Guru Ananda, hoping to bask in his presence as long as possible. They'd brought along large cardboard boxes full of cold bottled water. I gulped mine down in seconds. With nowhere to dispose of the bottle, I saved it. Perhaps I could use it to bring some sacred river water back home with me.

Brahmachari Jeevan had been sitting down and sweating profusely when Guru Ananda returned. He stood up to speak but immediately wilted back to the ground. He'd lost consciousness. Brahmachari Krishna leapt to his feet to come to the aid of his brother monk.

I made my way forward, hoping to offer some assistance. Seeing the monk right before he collapsed to the ground, I'd noted his face looked ashen and his breathing was haggard—the look of someone about to suffer a vasovagal syncope. It causes a person's blood pressure and heart rate to drop, which in turn causes fainting. It's usually triggered by a stressor like the sight of blood or lack of food. Or, likely in Brahmachari Jeevan's situation, heat exhaustion.

By the time I made it to the front of the crowd, Brahmachari Krishna had his brother monk's head in his lap and was stroking it like a concerned mother with a sick child. It was moving to see his affection. His local assistants ran through the parking area, shouting to each other about calling a doctor.

"Guru Ananda Ji, I'm a doctor," I said, adding the suffix to his name to indicate respect. "Please allow me to examine him."

The ever-tranquil guru, unruffled by all the commotion surrounding the drama, nodded his head. I procured a bottle of cold water from an anxious onlooker and splashed a few drops on the monk's face. My eyes scanned his chest, and I was reassured to see him taking deep breaths. I proceeded to check his pulse by placing three fingers from my right hand on his wrist and two fingers from my left hand on the carotid artery in his neck. His pulse was steady but slower than it should've been. My initial diagnosis was correct.

Brahmachari Jeevan's head was propped up in the other monk's lap, and his legs were straight out, but he needed the opposite. Gravity was draining much-needed blood flow from his brain. A hand popped out of the crowd offering a towel, which I folded and placed on the ground. While easing the monk's head onto the towel, I instructed Brahmachari Krishna to prop his brother monk's legs up in the air. Brahmachari Jeevan came around in no time, looking a bit confused at first but quickly sorting out his senses. His first action was to stand and bow to Guru Ananda, asking for forgiveness, but of course, there was nothing to forgive.

With the two Brahmacharis remaining inseparable for the time being, too preoccupied with Brahmachari Jeevan's health to assist Ananda, the group needed a new spokesperson. Someone to enforce the rules and take the head counts until we arrived safely at the ashram.

An American woman stepped forward and introduced herself as Marilyn, one of the three program volunteers. She had short curly hair the colour of India ink and was adorned in a pristine white silk sari. Her skin was pale like the petals of a Vendela rose. The harsh sunlight reflected off her, causing her to squint uncomfortably. Her eyebrows knitted together, and she didn't smile. I couldn't tell if it was because of the sun or if she was truly a serious person. I supposed I would find out soon enough; Marilyn was the new troop leader.

"Everyone, please settle down! We're already behind schedule. Let me get a head count, then we'll head to the Jeeps."

Tim and Jacques approached me with high fives, grateful I'd been able to help Brahmachari Jeevan. Until that point, I hadn't made it known to anyone I was a doctor—not even on the enrolment form for the retreat. I wanted that aspect of my life to lay completely dormant for two weeks. Why would I want to bring my work with me when I was seeking relief from the constant stress of my work responsibilities?

Finished counting, Marilyn turned to me and anointed me the team doctor.

"Any other doctors in the group?" she asked.

A slender man with an impish smile and a thinning ponytail put his hand up.

"What's your specialty?"

"I'm a naturopath and a homeopath," the man said, introducing himself as Jim. He then pointed to his suitcase and said, "I have my medicine bag with me, full of treatments for common ailments. Sore throats, sprains, bruises, upset stomachs, fevers, body aches, coughs…"

Marilyn's tight smile signalled acceptance of his credentials.

Guru Ananda eyed Marilyn and tapped his watch. We couldn't afford to waste any more time. She clapped her hands sharply to demand attention.

"Listen up! We are in a foreign country under extreme time pressure to get up the mountain. From now on, anything you need, you come to me. There are several Jeeps at our disposal. Each vehicle can seat nine people, including the driver. Set your luggage outside the vehicle you choose. Once everyone is seated, I'll go around again to make sure everyone is on board."

Brahmachari Krishna was overcome with the responsibility of supporting his friend, who, in my opinion, was taking too long to return to normal. Given his young age and relative health, he should've been feeling much improved by that point. Concerned, I stayed back to help them. Brahmachari Jeevan was taking slow, measured steps, releasing an occasional moan. As all the others rushed ahead to the Jeeps, I knew I'd be the last one to claim a seat.

I couldn't help but flash back to seventh grade when my school received a donation in the form of an elaborate band set. We couldn't agree on how to distribute the instruments fairly, so the music teacher made us race for them. He lined all the instruments up at one end of the soccer field and had the students line up on the other. If we reached the instrument we wanted before anyone else, it would be ours for the rest of the school year.

"On your marks," he said, raising his hand above his head. "Get set… Go!"

His hand flew down.

Everyone took off in a sprint for the instruments like an entire lifetime of happiness was at stake—except me. At that age, I was a tad undernourished. I also lacked any competitive drive to potentially compensate for my physical weakness. As a result, I surprised no one by being the last to cross the finish line. All of the desirable instruments—the trumpets, saxophones, clarinets, and cymbals—were taken. By the time I arrived, the only thing left was one large, ugly bass drum. During every school parade for the rest of the year, I was resigned to the fate of carrying that hideous drum. As I accompanied Brahmachari Jeevan to the Jeeps, assuming I would likely be left to occupy whatever undesirable seat remained, I could still vividly imagine the drum's large strap over my scrawny shoulders, its annoyingly low pitch booming in my ears.

As the monks and I approached the cars, the other group members were mingling around their luggage. Due to the excessive heat, the insides of the vehicles were broiling. Instead of reserving seats by staying inside, my retreat-mates had designated their spots in the form of hats, sunglasses, and books.

Already resigned to my lack of choice, I spotted one Jeep with a front seat completely empty of both person and proxy. Ha! I couldn't believe my luck. Without hesitation, I jumped inside to claim it. A few minutes of suffering in the hot interior was a small price to pay for the pleasure of a roomy, breezy window seat. There was even a cut-out under the dashboard, creating extra legroom. I was absolutely giddy to have found such a spacious sanctuary for both my long legs and my rucksack. Bonus: since it was up front, I had hope of taming my motion sickness. I was truly set, and everything seemed in order. I placed the rucksack on the floorboard between my legs and waited.

The driver approached and circled the Jeep, inspecting the tires. I'd noticed they were balding, obviously worn beyond a safe limit for the drive we were about to undertake. I was concerned, but the driver, on the other hand, seemed rather pleased the rubber was still intact.

The roads in the area were known to be treacherous. Fortunately, it was still too early in the year for monsoon clouds that far north. During the rainy season, Himalayan roads were famous for unexpected landslides. I fixed my eyes on a small Hindu idol glued to the dashboard—Ganesha, the remover of obstacles.

Fitting, I thought. Trying to make it up a mountain in an overloaded vehicle with bald tires? Ganesha's the one you want to hear your prayers. I felt slightly comforted and allowed myself to relax.

Brahmachari Jeevan, still recovering, spotted me sitting too comfortably in the front seat. He sprang back to life, shouting, "No! That is Guru's spot! You cannot sit there. You must find another place!"

He seemed rather annoyed with me, but at least he was feeling better. With no other choice, my rucksack and I stepped outside. Passing all the other vehicles, I saw no more spots available. Everyone was seated and ready to go. With the sun beating down and the Jeeps not yet moving, heads poked out of all the windows, trying in vain to catch a breeze.

Brahmachari Jeevan was standing guard at the guru's spot. Guru Ananda finally appeared, smiling as usual. The apprentice held the door for his teacher as he climbed into the Jeep and shut the door.

"Now you," the monk said. "Let's look for a place."

There were two vehicles designated for the women. Marilyn was in one of them, and they were both full. We returned to the vehicle I'd been offloaded from. A pleasant-looking gentleman was sitting in the seat behind Guru Ananda. He pushed open the squeaky door and told me there was a smidgeon of space left next to him in the back. I peered in and saw it—the inescapable middle seat, destined to become the bass drum of my spiritual retreat.

There was no room inside for my rucksack. It would have to join the cargo already piled atop the luggage rack, cinched down with thick coconut fibre rope. I had to ask the driver to help me undo the coarse knots and rearrange a few items. We sandwiched my belongings between two gigantic suitcases. My rucksack would be exposed to the elements, but at least it'd be safe.

I wondered what people were bringing to the retreat that required so many bags. There were nine people inside our vehicle plus several hundred pounds of luggage. Would we even be able to make it up a single mountain pass? The driver struggled to tie the ropes again, tugging one way, then the other. I tried to help, but I couldn't follow his methodology. He growled at me as I pulled hard when he was actually asking for more slack. He ended up recruiting a couple of bystanders to help, and together they accomplished the task.

Guru Ananda kindly advised the driver to hurry up, so he quickly returned to his seat and turned the key in the ignition.

The engine squealed in protest. Even when our driver twisted the key until it could go no farther, still no luck. He let the engine rest and tried again, pulling on a knob with his left hand while twisting the key with his right. His right foot was on the gas and his left on the clutch pedal. Engaging all his limbs to achieve the solitary act of coaxing the ancient machine back to life, I heard him utter a prayer to the gods.

Meanwhile, I was trying to grow accustomed to my cramped surroundings. To my right, the pleasant-looking gentleman introduced himself as Gustavo from Colombia. On my left sat broad-shouldered Hal from Australia. Behind me, where the back had been modified to hold bench seats, sat four women—two friends from India and a set of identical twins from Puerto Rico. The next eight hours would be a true test; I was already starting to feel clammy and dizzy. I hoped it was simply low blood sugar from skipping lunch and not claustrophobia lying in wait. Normally, claustrophobia isn't an issue for me, but every once in a while, it decides to pounce from the shadows and launch me into a tailspin. I thought about having to spend the entire day squeezed from both sides, and I began to pray it wouldn't be as bad as my experience ten years before.

I'd broken and dislocated my shoulder while mountain biking in Santa Fe, New Mexico. My friend, Greg, aided me during the gruelling two-hour walk down the rugged mountain path to his car. He drove me to the ER, where they manipulated my shoulder back into place and sent me for an MRI. I was fine until the motorised gurney pulled me into the confines of the machine. Once inside, my body flew into a full panic. I felt I'd been buried alive, and the unsettling, deafening noise of the whirring magnet made the MRI sound like someone was knocking on my coffin. Writhing around, I'd screamed for help. The MRI technician ran into the room. My vital signs weren't in range, and she feared the worst. It turned out I'd disconnected some wires, but it took four staff members and a sedative to calm me down. I prayed I would not have a similar episode in the Jeep. There were no sedatives in sight.

The driver tried to start the vehicle a couple more times. He said we'd probably have to wait a while since the engine was likely flooded from repeatedly pumping the gas pedal. I was so desperate to get us moving that I volunteered to give the Jeep a push start. Gustavo and Hal were happy to assist. With our combined efforts, we were able to push fast enough for the engine to roar back to life with a pop of the clutch. The engine sputtered, sending exhaust fumes into my lungs. I marvelled at my ability to become sick to my stomach before we even left the parking lot. After a few deep breaths, I squeezed back into my seat for the eight-hour road trip ahead.

Chapter 8

One by one, the convoy of Jeeps rolled out of the parking lot, turning north towards our destination town of Uttarkashi. The actual distance between Haridwar and Uttarkashi isn't too far—about one hundred and thirty miles. However, due to poor road conditions, frequent landslides, and heavy traffic, it's painfully slow going. Summer is the high season, with thousands of pilgrims, tourists, backpackers, and hikers traveling up and down the same route. Large trucks transporting heavy equipment for road clearing and hydroelectric projects are also prevalent.

Guru Ananda was conversing in Hindi with our driver, Hanuma. He lived in a village close to Uttarkashi and assured us he was quite familiar with the roads. He also had the contacts of several villagers along the way who'd promised to alert him about any unexpected detours or closures. GPS wasn't reliable, so having a trusted local was indispensable. The other drivers with our group were also from the area, which I found reassuring. In the event, something unpredictable occurred on our way up the mountain, the drivers would take care of us. I made a mental note to tip them well.

The mood in the Jeep was subdued. Perhaps it was on account of the heat, or maybe because there was a guru riding shotgun. I wondered how many of my fellow seekers felt intimidated by the presence of the spiritual master. After all, there probably wasn't much anyone could say that would impress or interest him. Why speak at all if, when the words spilled out, they sounded simple or foolish? I felt privileged to be in the presence of someone so wise and learned. The literal translation of 'Ananda' means bliss, and that man truly seemed to embody such a state. I thought about how he'd be sitting right in front of me for hours; it was my chance to observe and learn. I knew I might never get another chance like that, so I decided to covertly watch his every move.

We'd only been driving a few minutes when we received our first honour of the day—meeting the sacred Mother Ganges. The Jeep ventured over an expansive bridge that carried us high above her gracefully flowing waters. I looked on in wonderment, never before having seen the river in person. Dense traffic slowed us to a stop halfway across the bridge, and for a few minutes, we had a perfect vantage point to admire her grandeur.

Devout Hindus believe ritual bathing in the Ganges will wash them of their sins. I could see a mass of bodies below us, crowded along the riverbanks at *ghats*, the designated bathing areas with steps leading into the water. The current in the Ganges can be swift, so metal chains are anchored to the stairs to prevent people from being washed away. I watched with interest as hundreds of participants braved the strong waters. They pinched their nostrils shut with one hand, completely submerging themselves. With the other hand, they clung to the life-preserving chains.

The headwaters of the Ganges originate from a glacier high in the Himalayan Mountains. Despite being fed from a pure source, she's considered to be one of the most polluted rivers in the world. Fertiliser runoff, illegally discharged industrial chemicals, and sewage contamination continually threaten her health. Additionally, daily use by millions of people for bathing, washing clothes, and cremations compounds the problem. Regardless of severe pollution, hundreds of millions of people rely on her for drinking water and crop irrigation.

Hundreds of miles of the river are considered ecological dead zones, but in many areas, the Ganges and its tributaries are thriving. River dolphins, gharials, otters, turtles, and fish are some of the species that call her waters home. She's a true sustainer of life. With our minds, we have bestowed a sacred status upon her. Yet, with our bodies, we contribute to her demise. The Ganges is an unfortunate example of how people decimate the very resources they rely on for survival. This is a potentially fatal flaw of the human race. It will be telling to see if we can collectively muster enough awareness and will to save ourselves.

Heavy with thought, I said nothing until our approach to Rishikesh almost an hour later. The quaint riverside town is home to a stunning, immense statue of Lord Shiva the Destroyer sitting cross-legged in deep meditation over the Ganges. Shiva's title is somewhat misleading; he never destroys precious life—only the illusions, ignorance, and imperfections that accompany it. Millions of Hindus worship Shiva, believing the human spirit cannot evolve unless it continually rids itself of the negative aspects causing it to perform harmful actions.

I was very much hoping we'd have a reason to stop in Rishikesh. It's where the Bhagirathi and Alakananda Rivers join together to officially form the Ganges, creating one of the most ancient and holy pilgrimage sites for Hindus. Rishikesh is also well known for its abundance of ashrams, which offer teachings on different traditions of yoga and meditation. In the 1960s, the Beatles made this dot on the map famous to the entire Western world. They spent several weeks at the ashram of Maharishi Mahesh Yogi, composing music and learning Transcendental Meditation.

As the Jeep crawled along—sharing the road with humans, cows, dogs, horse-drawn carts, and automobiles—I visualised the Beatles singing throughout the streets of Rishikesh. I studied my surroundings intently, trying to download them to my memory. Tourists in shorts and tank tops commingled with modestly dressed Indian women. Clean, tidy priests wearing crisp white clothing walked among Aghori sadhus, whose naked bodies were covered with ash from nearby cremation grounds. I found it heartening to witness such a comfortable and easy mixing of people from so many different backgrounds and belief systems.

Continuing north out of Rishikesh, we encountered our first hairpin turn. I took a deep breath and a big bite of ginger candy I'd bought at the train station in Haridwar. Best-case scenario, the ginger would help stave off any motion sickness. Worst-case scenario, it would serve as my lunch. For another hour, we rode in complete silence. Guru Ananda's eyes were fixed out the window. I wondered what was going through his mind and decided it was time to initiate a conversation.

"Thank you, Guru Ananda, for giving us the opportunity to join you on this retreat," I said, hoping the others would also open up. I couldn't turn to see the Puerto Rican twins or the two Indian women sitting behind me, but they remained quiet.

"Wouldn't it be amazing to spend a few days in Rishikesh, learning about the different kinds of yoga?" gushed Gustavo with his ever-present smile.

Guru Ananda began to speak over the engine as it groaned up an incline.

"Yoga means 'union'. It cannot be learned in a few days. Our entire lives are spent in duality—happiness and suffering, war and peace, night and day, sweet and sour, and so on. Just as two rivers join to form the Ganges, the two arms of the nervous system must join together, creating inner peace."

I knew one facet of Guru Ananda's teachings focused on balancing energy flows in the body through Kriya Yoga. In addition to meditation, we'd be using his guidance on the retreat to deepen our own yoga practice. I'd dabbled in yoga off and on over the years, but I'd never committed to one particular tradition. Similar to my ongoing spiritual inquiries, I'd always dive in with an impulsive, scattered, and distracted mind. Buddhists call it 'monkey mind'. My wife calls it 'squirrel brain'. It's all one and the same.

Guru Ananda continued, saying, "You see that mountain in the distance? We are here, and there is the mountain. We see it as something separate from us. We may say, 'The mountain is beautiful. I am ugly.' But to a yogi's eye, there is no difference between oneself and the mountain. Both are manifestations of the same mysterious energy. Perfection in yoga means seeing everything as one."

It was hard for me to see myself in the mountain when its peaks appeared so cool and still, while I felt so hot and nauseous.

Guru Ananda must've read my mind. He went on.

"One adept in yoga is lord of the five senses. The senses are instruments of perception, not fingers to grasp at reality. The mind remains the master as long as we lean on our senses for experience. When you master your energies, the mind will have to listen to you."

"Imagine you have a hundred thousand rupees," he said. "You can spend them all at once on fleeting sources of entertainment, or you can save them and accrue interest. If you choose the latter, you can spend the interest on something useful without touching the principal amount. That is what Kriya Yoga is about. Conserving your energies, growing their power and intensity, and using those energies for the good of the world. There is no use for spiritual enlightenment if you don't have compassion for your fellow beings."

"There is so much suffering in the world. One person cannot alleviate all of it, but if each one does his or her own small part to help others, they will uplift the entire world. One thought cannot change the mind, but a collection of them can have a great influence. When you are in control of your sensual energies at all times, you control the source of your mind's energies as well, and no thought can arise without passing through your awareness."

Gustavo and I were deeply engrossed in the impromptu discourse. I glanced at Hal, who appeared to be uninterested, completely lost in his own thoughts. He was staring out his window. Guru Ananda fell silent again as the foliage along the road became dense. We were entering a forest of towering Sal trees. Considered sacred to both Hindus and Buddhists, every part of the tree holds value to humans. Preparations from its resin, leaves, fruits, and seeds are used for a variety of ailments across the subcontinent and beyond. It's even said that Buddha was born under a Sal tree. As we drove, the trees thickened. I was struck with the sudden urge to reach out and touch one, their spindly branches grasping vibrant green leaves that no doubt whispered blessings into the wind.

As we continued up the steep mountain at a steady pace of fifteen miles per hour, the air began to cool. I pepped up a bit and tried to engage Hal in a conversation. He didn't seem to know I was talking to him until I turned to face him.

"Sorry, mate," he said. "I was born deaf. I can't hear your words, but I can read your lips." There was a faint nasal twang to his voice, but if he hadn't told me he was deaf, I would've never known.

Once Guru Ananda realised Hal would not be able to read lips from a distance, he gave me the responsibility of providing Hal with detailed summaries of the daily talks. I was happy to be of assistance. After all, *seva*—service to fellow beings—is one of the pillars of Hindu spiritual practice. However, being confined to silence would pose a challenge. I wondered how accurately I could form words if I spoke to Hal by moving my lips with no real sound behind them. I decided it would be easier to take notes for him.

The road steadily led us farther up the mountain, continuing to carry us through wooded areas with dense vegetation. When the Jeep finally emerged into a clearing, Guru Ananda asked the driver to pull over at a scenic area so we could stretch our legs. A round man with a makeshift tea stall heartily encouraged us to buy a snack. Neither tea nor samosa would go easy on my stomach. I was barely holding it together and didn't want to be the reason for missing the checkpoint deadlines.

While everyone else was eating and drinking, I ambled off to enjoy the fresh air and soft sunlight that accompanies late afternoon. I felt content and strong in that moment, standing alone with no desire to be anywhere else. My mind was still. Guru Ananda appeared soundlessly at my shoulder, and we stood together, gazing into the endless expanse. The vista was breath-taking; surrounding mountains framed the deep valley with symmetrical perfection, and at the very bottom lay a delicately unwound ribbon of cerulean blue.

I suddenly felt the desire to impress the guru with my ability to stand in silence. I stiffened up a bit and locked my gaze on a distant tree. The practice got tiring rather quickly. I was hoping Guru Ananda would turn back so I could escape my self-imposed inactivity. What a silly game I'd set up. There was only one player. No one else had knowledge of my challenge. Who would move first—Guru Ananda or my ego?

He looked at his watch and whispered, "Time to go."

I'd won. Niranjan: one. Guru Ananda: zero.

As we made our way back to the tea stall, the other group members were scattered about, sitting on large rocks. Everyone was prattling on while leisurely sipping tea. Guru Ananda didn't seem too happy with the group's general lack of urgency. He had a word with the two young monks and Marilyn, and from a distance, it looked comical. Brahmachari Jeevan said something and pointed to Marilyn. Marilyn said something and pointed to the group. Brahmachari Krishna simply looked at the ground with his head bowed. Guru Ananda took matters into his own hands and shouted, "Come on! Let's go! This is not a picnic. It is getting late."

I walked back to the Jeep and circled around it, inspecting the luggage rack and the rope ties. If there was a weak link anywhere, the luggage could bust loose and tumble down the mountainside with my precious belongings. Everything seemed to be secure, but my rucksack was covered in a thick layer of sooty dust. No matter how clean the mountain air, we couldn't escape the trucks belching half-digested diesel.

We packed ourselves into the Jeeps, which had so far proven to be steadfast despite their various noises and rough appearance, and resumed our forward march to the ashram. I had no idea how much farther we had to travel, and I dared not ask. I refused to relay any indication of my discomfort and impatience to Guru Ananda. I was amazed at how well the other passengers were holding up. Gustavo's pleasant smile hadn't left his face since our first exchange. Hal had spent most of the drive silent, his head turned to the window, observing the exotic scenery. The Puerto Rican twins and Indian women had yet to speak in the presence of Guru Ananda.

I managed as well as I could to ignore my nagging hunger, persistent sweating, throbbing headache, and churning stomach. I reasoned if I could survive without complaint, I might advance one or two steps on the spiritual ladder. I vowed to keep my attention on some higher, abstract thought.

Not surprisingly, my focus on the profound was short-lived. I detected a new noise rising from the underbelly of the Jeep, one that went beyond its normal moans and groans. It started off as an innocent squeak but soon evolved into something coarse and offensive—metal grinding on metal. It was the brakes; they sounded urgently ill. I glanced at Hanuma. He appeared unconcerned.

While I debated whether or not the Jeep needed medical attention, my nose became distracted by the sudden savoury aroma of fried lentil crackers and sweet *Mysore Pak*. I was transported back to my childhood for a moment, remembering when my mom used to make the rare treat on special festival days. It contains generous amounts of ghee, roasted gram flour, jaggery, and freshly ground cardamom seeds. One of the Indian women asked me to pass two plastic snack containers forward to Guru Ananda.

It's customary in India to first offer food to the deity, the guru, and the elderly before everyone else takes their share. Guru Ananda blessed the food and gently set a piece of *Mysore Pak* with a few lentil crackers in a bowl made of dry leaves. He gave it to Hanuma. Only then did he take a single cracker and a piece of the sweet for himself. He handed the containers to me for distribution to everyone else. Hal declined; he said his stomach was feeling off after eating fried samosa. Gustavo took a generous handful of the crackers and two portions of *Mysore Pak*, his continual smile widening as he nodded his head in appreciation. I was undecided about eating. I compromised with a pass on the fried crackers but took the largest remaining piece of *Mysore Pak*. I couldn't resist. The ladies in the back polished off the rest.

The sugar intake from our unscheduled treat significantly lifted the mood in the Jeep. I asked the Indian women if they could sing bhajans, and Guru Ananda nodded in encouragement. They eagerly fulfilled our request. The singing was a welcome change of pace from the preceding hours of silence. The Puerto Rican twins each used an empty snack container to drum along with the beat of the songs. The rest of us joined by clapping. I hoped time would pass more quickly since we had some entertainment.

A few miles into our concert of devotion, the Jeep wobbled and slowed at an alarming rate—we had a flat tire. None of the other Jeeps from our group were within sight, either ahead or behind us. The road was narrow, and there was nowhere to stop without blocking traffic. We continued on a few hundred yards, looking for a suitable place to pull over. At last, Hanuma found a small spot to rest the weary vehicle. We all piled out on the side of the road. He jacked the car up and popped the offending wheel off in no time. Sheepishly, he turned to Guru Ananda and admitted he'd forgotten to pick up a spare tire in Haridwar. He quickly told us not to worry, as he knew most of the drivers taking passengers up and down the mountain. He would flag one of them down to borrow a tire.

We waited for about fifteen minutes before the next Jeep in our group caught up to us. The driver had a spare but wasn't willing to let it go. He suggested Hanuma try and solicit help from someone driving back down the mountain. After another fifteen minutes, Hanuma excitedly flagged down a passing Jeep. It was his cousin, Jayesh. They chatted a bit, and Jayesh happily offered his spare wheel. While the two of them were mounting the wheel, Jayesh noticed the problem with our brakes. The pads had somehow slipped out of place and weren't making proper contact with the rotor.

With no tools available to fix the problem, Hanuma was ready to ignore it and continue driving. Jayesh, on the other hand, was adamant and wouldn't let us proceed without some kind of repair. He told us there was heavy rain up ahead, and the roads were slippery. It would be much too dangerous to navigate the section with one reliable brake. The two of them discussed possible solutions and decided to look for a thin rope or string to tie around the pads to help hold them. They came up empty-handed.

I pulled down my rucksack and dug around, checking for anything that might be helpful. I found something and brought it to our provisional mechanics. Holding out my hand, I offered them my package of dental floss. Hanuma unspooled the entire roll and handed it to Jayesh, who wrapped it around the readjusted pads, securing them in place. I knew there was a good chance the floss wouldn't last very long once the brakes heated from friction, but I remained quiet. It was likely neither Hanuma nor Jayesh had ever seen dental floss. It was new material to them, and without field testing to prove its durability, they were willing to give it the benefit of the doubt.

Guru Ananda silently watched the exchange with a knowing smile. Perhaps he could see the future and was confident we'd reach the ashram safely. The sun was behind the mountains to the west; we were working in borrowed light reflecting off the clouds. Jayesh declared his surgery on the brakes a success, and we were on our way once again. Guru Ananda chuckled to himself and exclaimed, "We are now on Spirit Airways!"

God help us.

Chapter 9

I could hardly make out the weathered words on the boulder reading, "Uttarkashi: 10 kilometres." The Jeep's anaemic headlights were too weak to penetrate the accumulating fog. We turned sharply one way, then another, the tight bends escorting us up to the heavens. It was well past 9:00 p.m., and I was thankful the dizzying drop-offs and imposing mountains were no longer visible in the surrounding blackness.

It'd been terrifying to watch Hanuma manoeuvre around sharp corners in the daylight, often overtaking slower vehicles in the process. Numerous cars and trucks in much worse condition than ours had pitifully inched up the same road. In several spots, we encountered asphalt failures so extensive Hanuma asked Gustavo and me to get out so we could guide him around the deep trenches and jutting rocks threatening to halt our progress.

I never saw a single guardrail, not even along the steepest ravines. What I did see, though, was a section of highway on the opposite side of the valley that had completely vanished in a recent landslide. I prayed with a soul-shaking shudder that no one had been buried alive.

We'd been fortunate so far—other than the constant delays along the way. At one point, Hanuma unexpectedly pulled over, jumped out of the Jeep, and disappeared, running in the direction of a handful of huts in the valley below. Even Guru Ananda was surprised. Hanuma never mentioned why he was stopping or where he was going, but he was clearly in a hurry. He returned quite a while later with two locals. They informed Guru Ananda of a landslide ahead and advised us to turn back and take a detour through the valley and up again from another direction. Hanuma looked triumphant; he'd saved us from a probable overnight stop in the middle of nowhere. We backtracked and successfully avoided the area of concern, but the detour chewed up another hour and a half. Somehow, our entire caravan managed to stay together, so at least we would all arrive at the same time.

To my dismay, the ashram turned out to be north of Uttarkashi. By the time we found out, Gustavo had given up on being cheery and was sound asleep. Hal was trying not to nod off. I, on the other hand, was fully fuelled from jet lag, though my patience was on 'E'. It began to rain, and the temperature dropped precipitously. I found myself shivering and was suddenly thankful for the nine warm bodies stuffed cheek by jowl in the Jeep. Between the mediocre windshield wipers' rhythmic strokes, Hanuma was able to see just well enough to stay on course. Hopefully, we'd get to the ashram before the weather worsened. I closed my eyes and focused on my breath for the remainder of the ride.

By the time we slowed to a stop, the clouds had fully opened their taps, allowing for an unfettered downpour. I couldn't see anything out the windows, but Hanuma turned off the engine with such finality that I knew we'd reached our destination. He offered a silent prayer of thanks, hands folded over the steering wheel and forehead touching the top. We were anxious to get out, but we decided to wait for the weather to calm. Once the rain reduced to a steady drizzle, we finally emerged from the womb of the Jeep. To our left, I could see a steep mountainside covered in netting to prevent loose rocks from falling into the road. To our right was complete darkness, but I could hear the Bhagirathi River not too far away in a tearing rush to join its sibling, the Alakananda.

There was still work to be done before we could take shelter in the ashram, wherever it was. Hanuma, Hal, Gustavo, and I struggled to untie the tight, dripping knots in the cargo ropes. I pulled my rucksack down; it seemed unscathed, and it was clean again after its thorough shower. We unloaded the remaining luggage piece by piece. Finally, we stood with all of the bags around us, each one completely drenched.

Marilyn and Brahmachari Jeevan hurried between the vehicles, informing us in order to get to the retreat centre, we'd need to traverse the wide, barrelling river. Marilyn pointed everyone through the dark towards a long, narrow suspension bridge with gapped and crooked wooden slats.

"It's very old!" she yelled, trying to raise her voice above the roar of the water. "You'll have to go one at a time. Women first, then the men!"

As everyone haphazardly formed a line with their belongings in tow, a problem quickly presented itself. Many of the suitcases were too big to fit between the ropes fashioned as handrails. The luggage would have to be carried overhead for the entire length of the teetering, rickety bridge. Marilyn asked people to leave their luggage behind until we could figure out a safe way to get it all across. Instantly, a mini rebellion launched forth—the spiritual retreatants upset about being temporarily separated from the comfort of their material items. Marilyn was exasperated.

"Please, focus on getting across the river. We'll come up with a way to bring your things to you later. The bridge is wet and slippery—you need to be able to hold on to the ropes. We can't allow you to carry anything with you right now."

I was standing with Hal and Gustavo off to the side, observing the fit of unrest with a mix of amusement and unease. I had a feeling Marilyn was going to ask the three of us, along with the two remaining drivers, to be her solution for hauling the bags.

A lean, silver-haired man casually sauntered over to us from the midst of the upheaval. In a sunny tone antithetical to the situation, he chirped, "Hi, guys! I'm Len, from Dallas, Texas. How ya doin'? Wow, what an adventure so far. I've never seen anything like this. It's unreal! Where y'all from?"

Each of us greeted Len and summarised our respective lives in a few sentences. When the introductions were over, he stayed put. I wondered if I should warn him; I feared his proximity to us would make him the next member of the Unwitting Porters Club.

After a few minutes, the group—presumably tired of being cold and wet—surrendered to Marilyn in the battle of the bags. One by one, they crossed the bridge for the promise of dinner and dryness. As I expected, before crossing herself, Marilyn requested the four of us stay back to handle the bags. Then, without further plans or instructions, she faded into the murk.

I asked Hanuma in Hindi if he had any ideas about how to make our task easier. He told me not to worry; he'd already sent for help from a nearby village—may he be blessed one thousand times.

About forty-five minutes later, three villagers materialised out of the night air, each with a donkey in tow. The sweet animals had bells slung around their necks, making a jingling noise with each step. Hanuma told us the donkeys could each take several bags at a time on their backs. I picked up my rucksack and decided to carry it myself. I didn't want to trouble the scrawny Indian equines any more than necessary. The locals loaded the docile beasts of burden carefully, and each pair—animal and handler—made several trips back and forth across the bridge. I was amazed at how skilfully the donkeys negotiated the slick wooden planks as they trundled across the bridge.

When the last of the luggage had been delivered and everyone returned safely to our side, the four of us expressed our deep gratitude to the drivers and villagers. We were all exhausted, and our dedicated workers were eager to end their day. We bade them farewell. We wouldn't see them again until the return trip home. Hopefully, by then, the drivers would make another trip to Haridwar and have their vehicles examined and repaired. The thought of Hanuma going all the way back down the mountain with my dental floss as a key player in his Jeep's brake system worried me.

I was the last to approach the bridge. Grabbing the ropes tightly, I cautiously placed a foot on the one remaining obstacle standing between me and the retreat centre. I immediately deemed the situation untrustworthy. The structure swung side to side in the wind. It was nothing short of a miracle it'd withstood so much traffic in one go, and I worried the weight of the donkeys with their loads had been too much for it to handle. I imagined a frayed rope somewhere in the middle snapping before I reached the other side, plunging me into the frigid water below. Footing became my main priority. I couldn't afford to pull a Dr Bean and bust through a rotten slat, becoming stuck with one leg dangling until someone found me in the morning. Halfway across, the bridge dipped so low my feet got soaked by the wild current lunging at my ankles. I prayed to Ganesha.

Brahmachari Krishna, Hal, Len, and Gustavo were all patiently waiting for me at the far end. The monk said Guru Ananda and the rest of our party were in the main dining hall, and we were to report there right away. A plate of hot food, whatever it might be, was the only thing I wanted at that moment. I didn't care that I was soaked and shivering; I would deal with that later.

Len struggled to drag his suitcase up the hill through the mud, and he slipped several times. I took charge of his heavy load and continued to follow Brahmachari Krishna's faint outline. After stumbling about a hundred yards through the soggy, uneven terrain, we came upon the ashram's gate. Concrete pillars adorned both sides. A dim light hung above a small sign reading, "Welcome to *Tapovana*"—Sanskrit for 'Penance Forest'.

We entered the main building to find dinner in full swing. There were no chairs or tables in the dining hall. People were sitting on the floor, on steps, and on windowsills, holding their plates of *khichdi*—a simple preparation of rice and lentils. The servers were generous with their portions. I accepted three helpings on my plate and found a spot for myself in the room. A single bare lightbulb illuminated the blue walls and red floor.

Brahmachari Jeevan was patrolling the room with a clipboard, reeling off names and pointing in different directions to the various rooms. Sleeping arrangements were to be dormitory-style; a large room upstairs would sleep some of the women, and a small cottage down the hill, closer to the river, would provide room for a few more people. The meditation building was slightly up the hill but was off-limits for sleeping. The monk called my name and pointed to the small annex next to the dining hall.

After dinner, I went to my assigned sleeping quarters. The room was bare except for eight thin cotton sleeping pads laid out on the floor, leaving barely enough space down the middle to allow people to get to the bathroom. Plastic covers protected the scanty mattresses from dampness and mould. Brahmachari Jeevan told us not to remove them for any reason. We were each provided with a small woollen blanket, a miniature cotton pillow, and a bedsheet.

All the beds were spoken for except the one by the bathroom. Setting my bag down on it, I peeked through the bathroom door to find an Indian-style toilet—otherwise known as a hole in the floor.

"Ha!" I chuckled. "The Westerners will have fun with that."

I slumped onto my mattress. The limited light in the room came from the bulb in the dining hall. I couldn't make out who else was in the room, but I could tell Len was lying on the mattress next to me. He gave me a warm smile and a gentle nod before settling into bed. It was good to finally rest—the first program of the retreat would begin at 4:00 a.m.

Chapter 10

A reverberating clatter whisked me out of my dreams. Someone had tripped over my long legs and fallen into the metal bathroom door. Instantly, flashlights flicked on around the room. Their beams crisscrossed like infrared lasers in a museum, protecting priceless artwork from potential thieves. Everyone was awake. It was 3:00 a.m. Our first assemblage was in an hour.

Though we weren't allowed to speak, we managed to produce a variety of sounds in the form of grunts, yawns, *ahems* and squeaks from our gastrointestinal tracts. A line soon grew in front of the bathroom, and by 3:45, all of us were dressed and ready. The water to our bathroom came directly from the river and was biting cold, like the Bhagirathi itself. The absence of hot water was a great motivator to take expeditious showers.

I stepped outside, where faint moonlight reached through the scattered clouds. A muddy footpath led me up the small hill to the meditation hall. Most of the other participants were already sitting, their upper bodies wrapped in woollen blankets to warm themselves against the chill of the air. I wished I'd brought mine.

I chose a spot at the back of the room next to Len and eyed the interesting contraption he'd brought with him to use as a seat. It looked like an upholstered dining chair without legs. He noticed me checking it out, nodded with a knowing smile, and patted it with his hand. I returned his nod and smile, patting my small inflatable cushion. Hal spotted me and made his way to us, filling his bit of the floor with a long, firm, cylindrical bolster pillow. He took a seat, straddling it like a horse.

At exactly 4:00 a.m., Guru Ananda glided into the hall. He sat down cross-legged with his back upright and gaze fixed straight ahead. He smiled, his face illuminated in the soft glow of oil lamps sitting on the altar. He sat for a couple of minutes, perhaps sending silent blessings, then began the retreat with an invocation to the divine.

Om saha nau-avatu,
Saha nau bhunaktu,
Saha veeryam karavaavahai,
Tejasvi nau-adhiitam-astu maa vidvissaavahai,
Om shanti, shanti, shanti.
May we all be protected, may we all be nourished,
May we work together with great energy,
May we study together and let our study be effective,
May we not have jealousy or hate anyone,
Let there be peace in us, the environment, and the forces
acting upon us.

"Namaste and welcome," our venerable teacher said when he'd finished. He bowed his head and upper body, his hands pressed together, arms folded to his chest. "You have committed your time, energy, and money to come here. Thank you. Together, we will support one another and collectively lift our consciousness. This is a rare opportunity. Please do not take it for granted. Many of the junior monks in our order have not yet had the privilege of visiting and deepening their practice here. They are busy working in our orphanages, free health clinics, and schools."

I waited eagerly to hear his first lesson of the retreat. After sitting quietly for a few more minutes, he began.

"A baby comes into the world clenching both fists. A dying person leaves the world with both hands open. In between, we are busy doing this." He raised both arms for all to see and opened and closed his fingers of both hands several times. "We are continually grabbing and letting go of things until death forces us to let go completely. There is nothing physical we can take from this world when we die."

"Our hands hold on to material items, our minds hold on to experiences. We assign value to material items; we assign value to our experiences. We label them as good or bad, then tuck them away into our memories. When these experiences resurface, it's as if we are living them all over again. We drag out the past, again and again, and refuse to let go. This is one reason the mind can turn into such an unpleasant place—why the world can turn into such an unpleasant place. What would happen if we did not label or hold on to past experiences? We would not have such big problems in the world. No one would have reason to go to war. No one would have anger, or jealousy, or any of the other negative emotions that cause pain. None of you would be sitting in front of me now."

"When experiences arise, enjoy them, by all means, if they are appealing to you. But don't hold on to them at the cost of suffering. Even good memories can cause us to feel lonely or long for better days, so we must always focus on the present if we are to improve our current situation."

"We need to learn how to avoid forming permanent relationships with our thoughts. Can we form a permanent relationship with these mountains? No, we can't. We must enjoy them while we are here. If that enjoyment is total, we will be fulfilled, and when we leave, we won't have longing. In this way, whatever happens in your life, you can deal with it moment by moment. If something is bad, once it is over, do not bring it back. In letting go, you will progress quickly to reduce your suffering. The complete cessation of suffering leads to enlightenment."

"Meditation allows us to practice acknowledging thoughts then letting them go. Let us observe them without attaching labels—without clinging—and see what we discover about ourselves."

To signify the beginning of our meditation, Guru Ananda repeatedly chanted the ancient Sanskrit syllable, *Om*, used to balance and prepare the energies in the mind and body.

I closed my eyes, letting the vibrations of sound percolate through my body. I allowed myself to relax into the depths of my being, and for a few minutes, I experienced complete serenity. Then I found myself daydreaming about what might be served for breakfast. In an instant, my mind whipped up an entire mouth-watering feast, spending entirely too much time enjoying something that didn't exist.

I eventually shook free of my food fantasy. I was supposed to be letting my thoughts pass, not snaring them and tying them down. *What's wrong with me?* The next thing I knew, my mind was listing all my flaws. I was compulsive; I had very little common sense. I was thin-skinned; I was afraid

94

to say no to anyone. One thought after another unleashed itself until they created a buzzing swarm. I started swatting them down in my mind, but the imagery shook me so much I opened my eyes. I'd promised myself to keep them shut for the entire three-hour meditation, but I'd not made it thirty minutes. 'Pathetic'. I still had two and a half hours left to go.

With great difficulty, I brought my concentration back to the present moment.

Not ten minutes later, I had a profound realisation—my inflatable cushion sucked. I fully blamed its manufacturer for my rapidly increasing knee pain. Surely, the throbbing was the consequence of an unstable, low-quality product. I panicked. How was I going to spend hours each day sitting on such an inferior device? What if the stupid thing popped, snapping someone out of their momentous *samadhi*?

Before my mind could spawn a second or third generation of thoughts from the nonsense in my head, I returned awareness to my breath, trying to centre myself again. For a little while, it seemed to work—at least until I found myself wondering what the other people in the room were thinking. How quiet were their minds? Were they struggling like me? I envied Len's foresight in bringing along something that resembled a chair. Hal looked comfortable, riding off into bliss on his bolster pillow. My eyes darted around the room, and I noticed several people squirming on their respective mats and pillows. I reassured myself everyone was dealing with their own internal issues. Except Guru Ananda. He sat as unmoving as the trunk of an old oak tree, peace and calmness radiating around him like branches and leaves.

I reminded myself that the path to enlightenment is like driving. Stay focused on the road, ignore the distractions. But

I felt like most of the time I couldn't even see the road. When I was nine or ten, my brother Nagraj and I would sneak my grandfather's Morris Minor out for a drive around the block. Nagraj would sit in the driver's seat, steering and handling the gear shift. I would huddle on the floorboard and work the pedals with my hands. It took a lot of coordination, with Nagraj yelling out instructions on when to brake, when to clutch, and how much gas to give. We got pretty good at it and took the car out whenever we could. We got caught one day when my brother forgot to set the parking brake. The car rolled into the neighbour's wall. We scattered from the scene of the crime and spent a few days lying low at my cousin's house until tempers cooled. Whenever my grandfather went out of town after that, he would jack the car up and hide the wheels so no one could drive it.

My thoughts continued to bounce around, my mind full of self-doubt, my cushion low on air. I felt crammed on the floorboard, awaiting further instructions. I marinated in frustration until our teacher's voice came forth to bring the class to a close.

He told us to note all the sensations, thoughts, feelings, and physical discomforts we were encountering, but not to interpret or dwell on them. I noted my knees were throbbing, my lower back was sending electric shocks of pain down my legs, and my feet were lifeless. I dug a fingernail into the arch of my foot. Zero feeling. It would be a slow process to untangle my legs.

Guru Ananda ended our gathering with a long, drawn-out *Ommm*, then popped up, bowed, and floated out of the room with no indication he'd been rooted to the ground for the last three hours.

Upon his exit, people began to murmur. Marilyn slowly stood up and raised her hands.

"Shhh! Respect your vow of silence. If you need to communicate, write it down. There will be a question-and-answer session with Guru after the final meditation each day. We'll hand out paper and a pencil and allow one question per person. This is for spiritual inquiries, not complaints about the accommodations. If you wanted the comforts of hot water and feather pillows, you should've stayed back home. You are all budding yogis. Learn to accept. This is why you are all here."

Brahmachari Jeevan read through the day's announcements regarding mealtimes and other activities.

"Private study time is from one to three p.m. I have been to many retreats, and I have yet to see anyone come back to this room and meditate on their own. Most go to their rooms and sleep. I hope it will be different with this group. If you want to walk around outside, please stay close to the ashram. We don't want anyone to get lost in the surrounding hills and forests. At seven p.m., we will go to the riverbank and offer evening prayers to Mother Nature."

"Oh, one last thing," he added. "There were a few umbrellas left behind by the previous group. You may use them, but please return them at the end of the day to the blue bin by the front door. Now, please make your way to the dining hall for breakfast."

I could hear the steady pitter-patter of rain on the sloped roof. I was eager to get a view of the surroundings. We'd arrived in darkness the previous night. We'd entered the hall in darkness that morning, and the window shades were drawn. I was slow to get up. Len folded his chair and put it away in the corner. I deflated my air pillow and stuffed it into my pocket.

I followed Len out the door and drew in a sharp breath. The surrounding beauty was far beyond anything I could've imagined. We were at the highest point on the property, with the other two buildings not far below us. Downstream from the ashram, the river made a sharp turn, widened, and the flow became gentle. Upstream was a narrow valley with steep mountainsides rising on both sides. There, the current was swift, whipping up white foam as the water crashed around large boulders moored in the river. I then caught sight of the wooden suspension bridge we'd crossed the previous night. Tall support pillars on either side anchored the ends of the bridge, its centre bouncing dangerously in the increasing winds. Low clouds obscured the mountaintops. I wondered if there was a storm coming. I let my gaze wander, lost in the timeless setting. I was hungry but made no rush for the dining hall.

Breakfast was well under way by the time I arrived. The two volunteer cooks who'd accompanied us from Delhi were busy in the tiny kitchen. With a single wood-burning stove for cooking, feeding over forty people was a full-time job for them. It made sense why we had one simple dish for every meal. I didn't know the cooks' names, but I made sure to thank them as they served my food.

I'd taken more than my fair share at dinner the previous night, so that morning, I took one serving of rice flakes with peanuts and coriander. I chewed slowly and relished every bite of flavour. A cup of hot masala chai warmed my mood. I sipped my tea mindfully, imagining the steam rising to join the clouds. I felt content. What a contrast to the feelings of frustration I'd endured a few minutes earlier. If only it were so easy to slip into that state at will.

By the time I finished breakfast, the rain had picked up and was falling fast and steady. No one could escape the chill and dampness; it followed us everywhere, even inside the buildings. It permeated everything around us. I'd hung the last night's wet clothing on a clothesline strung across our room, but at that rate, it would take days for them to dry. I'd packed three sets of clothes, and my second set was about to get soaked through.

I decided I deserved an umbrella for my short trip back to the other building. The last thing I wanted was to start the next session feeling excessively damp. From the window of the dining hall, I spotted an umbrella on the patio, propped open and lonely. I grabbed it on my way through the door and strode up the hill. I was halfway to my destination when a short, plump, dark-haired woman came running out behind me, charging up the hill, waving her hands. She looked distraught. I looked around, wondering if she was perhaps trying to warn me of some impending danger. A bear or a tiger, maybe. She forcefully thrust her finger into the air at me, then pointed to herself. *What could she possibly want?* I thought. She continued to gesticulate in an increasingly frantic manner, and as she got closer, she reached out as if to pluck the umbrella from my hands. I shrugged my shoulders and handed it to her. She whipped out her smartphone and started typing.

This is my umbrella. I claimed it and set it aside to dry. You can't have it.

She spun around and hurried back towards the dining hall. She didn't even use the umbrella; instead, she closed it and clutched it under her arm like a protective mama bird sheltering her chick under one wing. I became resigned to the fact I was going to get wet no matter what I did. I silently thanked Umbrella Lady for teaching me a lesson from which I would eventually derive meaning and hurried the rest of the way to the meditation hall.

I wasn't particularly looking forward to spending another three hours on my cushion from hell. Len was already seated comfortably, deftly moving the prayer beads of a *mala* between his thumb and index finger. Hal was sitting next to me, mounted on his trusty steed. Pointing to my notepad, I did my best to indicate I would take notes for him. I'd forgotten to do so during the first meeting of the day, and I felt bad. It had to be difficult not being able to hear the lectures or follow verbal input during classes.

I resolved to write the cues in real time and show them to Hal. It would mean sacrificing my own experience, but I figured helping Hal would prove far more rewarding than being stuck with my own spinning thoughts. I'd also have some freedom to move and look around without getting in trouble.

Our dedicated teacher arrived at 9:00 a.m. on the dot and commenced session number two with another invocation to foster acceptance and unity. After his preparatory chanting, he closed his eyes and led us through a long guided visualisation. He described the birth of the Ganges, starting with its first drop of water, and took us on a journey of contemplation along the entire body of water until it met the ocean. I did my best to turn his words into sentences so Hal could create his own visualisations and enjoy the experience. Len had closed his eyes and leaned back into his chair, stretching his legs out in front of him. He continued to move the prayer beads through his fingers, indicating he was in his own little world. He stayed that way during the entire class. *He must be an advanced practitioner*, I thought.

Since my stomach was full, it was much easier to focus during meditation. My mind continued to wander, but I did a much better job of not getting tangled up in the thoughts.

Guru Ananda brought the session to an end by saying, "Entering the depths of meditation to advance our own self-realisation while ignoring the cries of fellow humans in need is not spirituality. We must balance our practice with service to others. Heaven and hell are right here on earth. Once we are armed with the knowledge of how to liberate ourselves from the grips of suffering, it is our responsibility to share that information with others."

A final *Om* signalled the end of the session. It was time for lunch.

Chapter 11

I wanted to explore. It was after lunch and three hours until tea time. I remembered Brahmachari Jeevan's warning not to stray too far from the ashram, so I set two goals for myself. First, survey as much of the surrounding area as possible. Second, do it without getting lost. I plopped down on my mattress to put on my hiking boots. Len was stretched out in his bed, lost in a book. I couldn't see the title, but he was furiously underlining sentences and making notes in the margins. I was impressed with his dedication.

Making my way outside, I wondered what everyone else planned to do during free time. Jacques, Tim, the Puerto Rican twins, and Jim were headed for the ashram's main entrance, presumably to admire the river. I decided to go the opposite direction—up the mountain. The only thing I felt like taking with me was my camera, which was tucked safely in a plastic bag. The rain had paused as if honouring a cease-fire, but I didn't trust it to stay that way.

I scanned the property, examining my options for egress. The ashram sat on a relatively small, isolated parcel of land. Right behind the meditation hall stood a towering, sheer rock face, smooth and covered with moss. I had doubts even an experienced climber could scale it successfully. Hoping to locate a viable launchpad for my expedition, I continued searching. I was soon rewarded at the far end of the ridge—a narrow trail pointed upstream, leading into the woods. Without hesitation, I set off.

After a few minutes of easy walking among the trees, I came upon a small clearing. It was brimming with stepped terraces, an abundance of crops growing in each one. I wasn't sure what kind they were, but more than one type had been planted together. The farmers were taking advantage of the symbiotic relationship between species in order to increase crop yields. They were also maximising limited space. Very little land in the area was available for cultivation due to the steep hills, rugged ground, and poor soil.

I continued on the path before me, which soon cut through a collection of small, brick huts with thatched roofs. The women tending the little village wore vibrant cotton garments. Children ran about, playing their version of tag. I didn't see any men; I assumed they'd commuted to the valley below for work. Goats, sheep, and cattle roamed freely around the dwellings, on the path, and down the mountainside. The villagers smiled as I waved to them. They seemed content. They had everything there they needed. I admired their self-reliant existence.

The trail wound uphill through another section of dense forest. Eventually, I emerged into a second clearing with another small, terraced cultivation. Crouching amid the crops was an elderly woman, absorbed in her task, harvesting vegetables. She moved stiffly down the row, her weathered hands working the plants. She took notice of my presence and offered a gentle smile. Her brown eyes radiated kindness, but they also held something deeper within them. Sadness, perhaps? I wondered what joys and sorrows she'd experienced in her long life. It was entirely possible she'd never left the village and didn't care what lay beyond. From her garden, I could see back down the valley all the way to the ashram and river.

It was not yet time to turn back. I forged ahead. The climb suddenly became steeper, rockier, more arduous. It took me out to the edge of the mountain. The wind blew in cool gusts. Mist lay heavy in the air. In no time, my hike had transformed into a leg-busting climb, and my lungs were fighting the effects of the high altitude. The challenge was starting to become more than my body could handle, and though I knew my muscles would probably regret it later, I wanted to find out where the path was leading me. I hadn't encountered any splits in the trail, so I knew I'd have no problem retracing my steps back to the retreat centre.

I heard voices approaching from behind. Several women and children appeared around the bend. The women were hunched over and had large bales of hay strapped on their backs. Despite the extra weight, they were walking twice as fast as I was and passed me easily. The children jumped and skipped along the steep incline, following their mothers. The thin air didn't bother them at all, their bodies perfectly acclimated to the altitude. I watched the group advance until they were gathered by the mist, one by one.

I continued trudging up, up, up, until my legs revolted. I dropped wearily onto a boulder that was protruding from a switchback. It was perched on the edge of an overlook, but the blanket of fog that enveloped me made visibility poor. Since I couldn't see outward, I closed my eyes and looked inward.

I pictured myself floating down the river below, letting the steady current carry me all the way out to sea. I imagined how difficult and draining it would be to swim against the stream, then realised that's how too many people tend to move through life. Attempting to control the actions of those around us is like demanding the river flow in the opposite direction to accommodate us. Life would certainly be less exhausting if we stopped fighting against the current and only used our energy to avoid getting caught up in things that threaten to drown us—like negativity and hatred.

Following that same line of thought, I wondered what it would take to simply allow my thoughts to flow effortlessly in meditation like the downstream current. What would happen if all my efforts in meditation became non-efforts? Would that lead me closer to accepting things as they are?

I'd been sitting quite a long time, remaining very still on my rock. When I opened my eyes, the fog had lifted. I beheld an incomparable view. Downstream, I could make out a dam in the distance. Upstream, a deep, green valley spread itself at the feet of soaring mountains. Nearby, a gently cascading waterfall disappeared into the trees below. From what I could tell, there was no way to leave the ashram other than the bridge. I saw no roads whatsoever on my side of the river. It confirmed my suspicion that the local villagers travelled everywhere on foot.

I should've turned around to go back, but a bit farther up the trail, I spotted a small temple. The building was old, made of brown brick, and painted red. On its roof, little orange and yellow flags danced in the wind. There was no door; anyone could enter. The temple itself was tiny, just big enough to house a divine statue. There would be no priest there.

I felt an urge to pay my respects at the solitary temple. Squeezing into the limited space between a crumbling wall and the stone deity, I instantly recognised it as Varahi—one of the mother goddesses. She's depicted with the head of a boar, often holding weapons capable of dispelling evil forces. The temple's idol was dark in colour, its features intricately carved. She was adorned with fresh flowers. *The local villagers must visit frequently*, I thought. I plucked a single wildflower from nearby and placed it at her feet. With my hands folded in prayer, I sought her protection and blessings before setting off down the mountain.

As planned, I returned to the dining hall with plenty of time to enjoy my afternoon chai. Samosas were served, and I was tempted to load my plate but reminded myself of the promise not to take more than I needed. My mind would have to learn to be content with 'enough', not 'more'. I'd already witnessed how difficult it was for the people of the region to grow food for themselves. They didn't have electricity, indoor plumbing, or vehicles to make their lives easier. I was fortunate to have my meals served on a plate, ready to eat.

After tea, on my way to the meditation hall, it occurred to me that I'd made it back just in time. Ominous clouds unfurled above me and began to spit hard rain. The sky grew darker by the minute, even though it was mid-afternoon. The storm had arrived. I was concerned by the amount of rain that had already fallen since we arrived. The river below us was swollen. I took comfort in knowing the dam downstream could assist with flood control—the sluice gates would be ready to open at a moment's notice should the waters rise too high.

Darting inside, I settled into my comfortable space between Len and Hal, then handed Hal the rest of the notes I'd taken during the morning session. I'd scribbled a few lines at the end about my hike. He seemed intrigued. I wanted to go again the next day and wondered if he might join me.

Chapter 12

"Why do we take a vow of silence?"

Guru Ananda posed the question at the beginning of the evening session.

"This morning, I saw some of you communicating through your phones," he continued. "Not talking, but typing notes to each other. This is the mischievous mind at work, always looking for a way to express itself. Meditation teaches us how to turn the expressive energy of our minds into spiritual energy. We cannot do this if we continually focus our energy outward. How much of our daily effort is spent in mindless gossip or constant texting? Silence is one of the best ways to help us focus inward, but many of you are losing the chance to do that by maintaining communication."

I had a difficult time hearing his words. The rain was pounding the roof, creating a steady roar. The front door was sitting open to reveal a translucent wall of water battering the ground. It felt like we were huddled in the undercut of a waterfall. I thought of the villagers, their roofs made of bundled plant material, and wondered how much protection their shelters afforded from such merciless torrents.

Guru Ananda was unfazed.

"From the perspective of the material world, this isolated place in which we sit is a dead end. It is no accident we chose to hold the retreat here. Lack of worldly distractions will force you to look within yourself. Who knows what tomorrow may bring? Nothing in the future is guaranteed. I implore you, for these next two weeks, to make the best use of this precious chance. It is not for my sake I am asking you to do this. It is for your benefit. No one forced you to come here. You came voluntarily. Perhaps each of you has a different expectation. For some, this expectation may not be met. For others, it may be exceeded. But why hold expectations at all? Why keep them as ruler against which you measure your happiness, your life, your worth?" He paused, letting his words soak in.

"When end results are not in line with our expectations, disappointment abounds. Unhappiness. There are seven stages in the grieving process, with acceptance being the final step. In spirituality, acceptance is the first step. Once we are in full acceptance, we can understand things as they are."

A violent blast of wind slammed two big windows open at the back of the room, sending the rain in sideways. We all scooted forward, trying to stay dry and straining to hear our teacher. I found the cosier atmosphere to be comforting; although we didn't know each other well, I imagined a bond forming between us as a result of our common interest.

Guru Ananda continued. His tone remained calm and steady, but the voice of the storm buried his words. I gave up straining to hear him, instead allowing the sounds of the storm to lead me in meditation. Unexpectedly, my choice triggered numerous raw emotions to rise in my mind. Hidden traumas and angst welled up, taking centre stage. Past antagonists in my life suddenly appeared to test me. I struggled to silence them, hearing their taunts in every groan of the storm.

I'd like to think I fought my demons into surrender. I'd like to say the strange chemistry between the relentless rain and powerful wind created a rhythm that placed me in a trance. In reality, I nodded off. When the *Om* sounded to signal the end of class, it seemed as if no time had passed.

Rain doused the ashram grounds in spurts. Despite the severity of the storm, we hurried to the riverbank to offer our respects to Mother Nature. What better time to honour her than when she's displaying her strength?

Decaying steps led down to a concrete platform above the water. It measured about five feet across, with a small square cut in the middle, revealing the river below. The opening made it safe to reach through and get our hands wet. Guru Ananda set a paper lamp adrift. It disappeared in a flash, snatched by the thrashing waves. One at a time, we knelt on the platform and extended an arm through the hole, connecting to the river with our fingers. Then we hurried to the dining hall for dinner.

I ate in a daze. I was cold again. Wet again. And completely spent. The effects of my ambitious afternoon hike combined with several days of inadequate sleep had finally dragged me past the end of functionality. After the question-and-answer session with Ananda, I'd be free to welcome a good night of sleep.

In the meditation hall, Brahmachari Jeevan passed around a basket to collect all of our questions for the guru. With great flourish, he shuffled the various paper scraps together as if tossing a spiritual salad. Despite feeling like I already had one foot in a dream, I was looking forward to discovering what astute questions my peers had posed.

Suddenly, we were interrupted by several blinding strobes of lightning, accompanied instantly by multiple cracks of sky-splitting thunder. Those instigators of fear tore through the air around us, shaking the core of the meditation hall. Everyone in the room instinctively made themselves smaller, and all our eyes became fixed on the open door, watching for whatever else was to come. It was obviously far more than a typical storm, and the ashram was in the heart of it.

Guru Ananda waited for some of the commotion to clear, then began.

"The first question asks: What is the importance of rituals, such as repeating a chant or mantra a specific number of times? I am not inclined to practice rituals. Will I still progress spiritually?"

He pondered the question for a few moments. Even though Guru Ananda was punctual with our schedule down to the minute, he never actually seemed to be in a hurry about anything. "The moment we say the word 'ritual', we usually associate it with religious observance. Each religion has its own prescribed order of practices or rituals. Yet, life itself often unfolds as one big ritual. It has a prescribed order from birth, youth, adulthood, death. At each stage of life, we act differently, and we create smaller rituals within those stages. For children, it may be playing. For adults, it may be working. For those in retirement, it may involve golf."

"There are smaller rituals within this broad framework of life, like celebrating birthdays, participating in hobbies. Many of these rituals in daily life are done without much thought or examination—as a habit. When everything is going well in life, it is easy to be lulled into a thoughtless, easy way of living. But we know life is not always smooth. There are hardships that create unpleasantness in the mind. These obstacles ensure we no longer go about our lives without paying attention. We begin to live more consciously, albeit in misery. The mind becomes restless or dissatisfied, and it seeks an escape."

"We may then turn to a new ritual for relief. Some people take to drinking, which then becomes a ritual to help settle the mind. Others may choose to adopt prescribed rituals from a religion that appeals to them. There is a hidden expectation that doing such things will bring happiness or restore the mind to a calm state. Anything done with focus and attention has transformative potential.

"Used correctly, rituals can be very helpful in smoothing the grooves in which the mind travels, but we must be intelligent enough to know when and how to use them and when to drop them. They can help us live consciously and grow in awareness, or they can become a crutch and hold us back."

Glancing at his watch, Guru Ananda said, "We have time for one more question." He picked a folded piece of paper gently out of the basket and read, "How do I overcome sadness?"

Again, he took his time in answering. "We cannot see the electricity we use in our homes, but we see evidence of its existence through light from a lightbulb, sound from a radio. It's the same electricity powering different items. We can turn the switches off, but the electricity supply remains unaffected because the source originates from somewhere else."

"Similarly, the mind's energy is like electricity. Sometimes this energy powers happy thoughts, sometimes it powers sad thoughts. The amazing thing is, we have control over our own power source—the mind. Sad thoughts don't have any power unless we supply the energy. If we turn off the switch, negativity can no longer grow in our minds. We can learn to control the switch."

"Learning how to do this may take some time. The next two weeks are a good opportunity for you to face challenging thoughts. Let them come into your mind and observe them without judgment. Don't suppress them or cling to them or react to them. Remain neutral and see what they do. After a while, you will find they start to dissolve, to fade away. I am here for support. We are all here for support. You are not alone. No one can claim they have no sadness. Everyone battles their own in one form or another. The key is learning to control the switch."

He checked his watch once again.

"It is past nine o'clock. Let's wrap up for the day. We will meet again at four."

And with that, he said the closing chant of the day.

Om sarve bhavantu sukhinah,
Sarve santu niraamayaah,
Sarve bhadraanni pashyantu,
Maa kashcid-duhkha-bhaag-bhavet,
Om shanti, shanti, shanti.
May all be happy,
May all be free from illness,
May all see what is auspicious,
May no one suffer,
Peace, Peace, Peace.

Chapter 13

The storm lashed the ashram with so much force we were afraid to leave the meditation hall. There would be no more breaks in the rain. No more pauses. No more cease-fires. Three or four at a time, we dashed out into the blackness between lightning strikes. It was as if the clouds themselves were nothing more than sieves, and water was draining through them from some unknown place beyond. We were being bombed with hurricane-force winds, lethal lightning bolts, and deafening thunder. Were the heavens waging war on us? The ten-second sprint from the meditation hall to the safety of my room had me praying for my life with every step. I made it safely. Dripping, trembling.

I had one set of dry clothes remaining. My plans to change once I got back to the room were short-lived. Flying debris from the wind had shattered several windowpanes in our room, and the rain had been blowing in for quite some time. Everything was sopping. Most of the mattresses were wet, their plastic covers beaded with rainwater. Several of the blankets—including mine—had soaked up the spray whipping through the air and were rendered useless. I had a chill in my bones I couldn't shake, and there was nothing I could do about it.

I turned to Len, who was busy piling on a sweatshirt and coat. He'd brought an abundance of clothes, all perfectly dry in his giant, hard-shell suitcase. I had nothing to add to my thin scrub pants and long-sleeve T-shirt. I hadn't even brought a light jacket or a raincoat. I'd packed very little for the trip, mainly for the convenience of carrying a single bag, but I'd also grossly overestimated my ability to withstand the dramatic Himalayan weather. Perhaps I'd watched too many documentaries with yogis living in the high peaks wearing nothing more than a wispy cloth covering. And it wasn't just the cold—my body ached from head to toe. Thinking of the warm comforts of my home and family, I suddenly felt homesick. I cursed myself for holding such high expectations for the trip.

The storm raged on for hours. I felt like I was stuck in a tiny ship lost at sea, and the only thing I could do was wait for the obliteration of my vessel. Lightning flickered every few seconds, allowing me a glimpse of my roommates. Most of them were sitting against the walls, trying not to look scared. I longed to speak to Len but didn't want to break my vow of silence twice in one day. My teeth were chattering. I decided to lie down on my mattress, hoping to generate a meagre amount of heat by curling up into a ball.

I had no doubt mass destruction was occurring all around us. Mixed in with the natural sounds of rain, thunder, and wind were constant eruptions of unfamiliar cracking, splitting, and crashing. At one point, a horrifying rumbling noise consumed us, and I felt the floor shaking and shifting. I envisioned the mountains crumbling around us, fully expecting our mother to open her mouth and swallow us whole. I shut my eyes tightly, waiting for it. It didn't come.

The rumbling eventually stopped, and so did the floor's trembling movements.

I could hear something else. The river's violence had reached a crescendo, the water's roar echoing the crash of epic sixty-foot waves on Maui's north shore. Except, we were nowhere near the beach. Somehow, within the storm and wreckage, fatigue overpowered me, and I drifted to sleep amid the restless elements.

I woke with a start at 3:45 a.m., fifteen minutes before the first meditation of day number two. Len was sound asleep, but everyone else had left the room. The wind had died down. It was dark and quiet. I'd probably slept two hours at the most, and I was tempted to shut my eyes again. Gathering every ounce of willpower, I stood up. Len was in a deep slumber, but I didn't want him to get in trouble for missing class. I gently shook his legs. He didn't respond. I tapped him on the shoulder. Nothing. Finally, I pressed two fingers into the middle of his chest. The sternal rub—a technique used by doctors to check a patient's sedation level—never fails. Len's eyes popped open. He looked startled and confused. I was a silhouette at the edge of his bed, standing motionless like an apparition. I broke the code of silence.

"It's okay. It's me. We're late for meditation."

Len was up in an instant and decided to forgo a shower—after all, he'd spent most of the night getting washed by rain. We hurried through the dark in our damp clothes, up the hill to the meditation hall. Marilyn was waiting by the entrance, scanning the area with a flashlight, a look of grave concern on her face. We were the last ones to arrive.

As we took our familiar places in the back of the room, Guru Ananda entered. He quickly sat and spoke immediately.

"Let's discuss uncertainty. And how best to deal with it when comes without warning."

I wasn't sure if he was referring to last night's storm, but finding Marilyn outside so early in the morning suggested something was amiss. Perhaps she and Guru knew something we didn't. Would they tell us that morning? Probably not. Once morning light spread over the eastern horizon, we'd be able to see the wake of the storm for ourselves.

"The only predictable thing about life is its unpredictability, and the mind does not like that. The mind prefers habits. Habits are like puddles. The water is shallow, the bottom visible. We do not fear walking through a puddle. Habits keep us in the shallowest parts of the mind, and they allow us to live with certainty. There is little fear when everything seems certain."

"Why, then, embrace uncertainties?" he asked us. "Because we cannot remain forever in our familiar world of shallow habits. By utilising the unknown, life is good at shaking us out of our comfort zones. New anxieties and fears take hold, and unless we become comfortable exploring our inner depths, there is nowhere safe to shelter."

"The good news is, by nature, we are all explorers. A few hundred years ago, much about the world was unknown and out of reach. Once sea routes were discovered and airplanes invented, humans insisted on exploring everything the world had to offer. Then what? We turned to the moon and put a flag there."

"Humans are curious beings. We want to investigate outer space because of its vast mystery. Now, consider there is also a vast mystery within us. Our mind has many layers, the depths of which we barely know. Our conscious mind is like the surface of a large lake. It can be still or choppy. It easily reflects our moods. But what if we go deeper? Approaching that unknown space is like entering a deep lake. We can't see the bottom, and we know there may be dangers lurking below. Yet, those who are brave enough to explore such depths do not carry their fears with them. They leave them at the surface."

"When we close our eyes and dive into the deep waters of our mind, our lake appears to be a void. To let our attention dwell there can be unsettling. We don't know what we will encounter. It is common for people to want to quickly open their eyes and return to the familiarity of the outer world, but there is only so much the outer world can teach us about our inner selves. The rest has to come from looking within."

Waving his hand in the direction of the river, he continued.

"The river is calm one day, destructive the next. Soon, it returns to its previous state. This is just like the mind. One moment it is peaceful—an easily liveable place—but the very next instant, it experiences a storm of anger, greed, or jealousy, destroying lives. But remember, this destructive force can only operate if it has an energy source. We can keep the surface of our lake from becoming choppy by not churning the depths with a response. We must step back and allow the storm to pass. Then we can safely return to peace. To still waters."

"No matter what we find outside, please keep your focus on why you came here. To learn how to be centred in the midst of the unexpected."

His face gave no indication of worry, but the mood in the hall had changed. Nervous energy was palpable. People were fidgeting and looking at each other.

"Let us meditate now," Ananda said.

I knew we were safe at that moment, but I couldn't concentrate. I closed my eyes, instantly reliving each horrible sound from the previous night, every minute of helplessness. I didn't want to sit quietly with my thoughts. I felt trapped. If I could sleep, maybe I could turn off the switch. But that was out of the question. A group meditation was in progress. I couldn't leave. Even if I did, where would I go? Back to the cold, damp room to sit on the slick plastic cover of a hard mattress? At least the meditation room was dry, and the body heat made it relatively warm. I resorted to taking slow, deep breaths, but a combination of fear and curiosity continued to fuel my restlessness. I gave up and opened my eyes. Guru Ananda was sitting with grace, steeped in absolute surrender. I felt ashamed of my mind, but all I could do was sit, stare, and wait impatiently for the final *Om*.

Chapter 14

"As you are all certainly aware, there was a huge storm last night," Marilyn began. The moment our meditation ended, she had hurried to the front of the room. "It was completely unexpected. None of the weather reports we saw before leaving Delhi provided any clue it was coming. There's no cell reception here, but we do have a satellite phone with a limited number of minutes. We made a brief call to our headquarters, and the monks there apprised us of a situation."

Marilyn paused, making eye contact with each of us.

"There has been a devastating flood," she said. "It's too early to tell the extent of the damage, and we don't know how long the rains will continue. After breakfast, please pack your belongings. We may need to evacuate. You have permission to break your silence, but keep the talking to a bare minimum. We'll let you know when we get more information."

It was almost seven in the morning, and night was yielding to day. We would be able to see for ourselves what had transpired overnight. As soon as Guru Ananda left the meditation hall, there was a mad scramble for the door.

"Whoa," Len said. "Let's wait for everyone else to clear out."

"Yeah, no sense rushing to the back of the crowd," I agreed.

I was relieved to finally be able to talk to him, the vow of silence no longer a barrier between us. We watched the clot of people push through the door and fill the narrow patio in front of the meditation hall.

"What a turn of events, huh?" Len said. "The trip of a lifetime over before we even got to the juice of it, you know? I sense a major shift in people's energies—their fear consciousness has surfaced. You and I, we should stick together. Stay positive."

Len didn't sound worried at all.

As we took our turn leaving the comfort of the meditation hall, it became clear it wasn't the same world we'd walked through the day before. The first thing I noticed was the river. It was practically at our feet. Giant waves slammed against the new riverbank carved into the earth just a few yards from where we stood. The steps and concrete platform where we'd offered oblations had disappeared far underwater. The channel was much wider, too, but the river looked different in another way—like its actual course had shifted. *Is that even possible?* I wondered. The current was swift and turbulent. Entire trees rushed by, tossed around like tiny twigs, snapping in half as they crashed into boulders. Then I looked for the bridge.

It was gone.

My eyes traced the river upstream to see what else had changed. Yesterday, on the opposite bank, I'd seen a village. It was no longer there. With a sick feeling in my stomach, I realised it had been washed away during the night. After all, the river was actively swallowing everything in sight. A lone two-story building sat a few yards upstream, also on the opposite bank. The day before it had been a normal, sturdy building made of brick, stone, and cement. That morning its beaten foundation balanced at the very edge of the water. I knew it wouldn't last much longer, and not five minutes later, the remaining bank beneath it gave way. The entire structure was sucked into the churning river, slowly broken apart, and carried downstream. With everything around us destroyed or flooded, there was no explanation as to how we were still standing on solid ground, alive and intact.

Not wanting to miss my chance to document the destruction, I went to the annex to grab my camera. I shoved in a new battery and ran back to the meditation hall. In the scene outside, the mind-numbing, destructive power of nature was on full display. Breakfast was no longer on anyone's mind. People were frozen in place, jaws open, eyes transfixed on the mayhem in front of us. Even the face of the mountain several hundred yards upstream was unrecognisable. The day before, it had been completely covered in dense foliage. That morning it was barren. That was the cause of the tremors during the night—the entire mountainside had broken loose and crashed into the river.

I turned to examine the rock face behind the ashram. It glistened in the morning light, standing sturdy like an impenetrable shield. That was one reason we were still alive. It had kept the mountain from coming down on us.

Except for the continual roaring of the river, things were silent. We must've stood there for over an hour, all of us speechless with disbelief. No one could move away from the destruction. It was as if the wreckage had a gravitational pull. Somehow, standing there became a deeply meditative experience. My mind was clear, my body weightless. I had nothing but complete awareness of the moment.

The clouds started to thin, but a light rain continued. Hopefully, we'd been through the worst of it, but I feared there would be more to come. Marilyn had stressed the fact we might need to evacuate that very morning, but I didn't see how it could possibly happen. We didn't yet know if there was a way out by land, and the waters were too rough to navigate with a boat of any kind. I balked at the thought of slamming into the sluice gates of the dam downstream. It didn't seem like there was anywhere nearby for a helicopter to land. There was no longer any flat ground by the river, and the remaining riverbank was extremely unstable. The high altitude, unforgiving wind, and steep slopes of the mountain range would make it extremely risky for helicopters to come anywhere near us. I knew we were trapped, but I decided not to share my conclusion with anyone at that moment. I didn't want to create a panic.

"Okay, let's go." Marilyn and Brahmachari Jeevan ushered everyone in the direction of the dining hall. "More announcements will be made soon."

Breakfast was cream of wheat with Indian spices, served with masala chai. What a blessing to have hot food. I thought of the villagers I'd encountered the previous day on our side of the river. How had they fared during the storm? Their crops were undoubtedly destroyed. Had their huts survived? Had they survived? I suddenly lost my appetite. At the ashram, we had strong roofs and walls to protect us, and our livelihoods weren't tied to that place. We would be able to leave everything behind and return to the safety and comfort of our daily lives. But what about the people who called the area home?

From the vantage point on my hike the previous day, I'd studied the lay of the land. The neighbouring village was several hundred yards upstream, where the valley narrowed considerably and the mountains grew taller. Downstream, the river turned away from us, leading to the dam. If the dam had been breached, there would be incalculable losses. Both people and property would be affected for miles. Whoever survived would likely be homeless. The worries we faced at the ashram were minor in comparison, and I was deeply grateful to be alive. I repeated a mantra until my nerves calmed down. 'Accept. See how things unfold. Take one moment at a time'.

"I have important information!" Marilyn had reappeared in the middle of breakfast. "Please pay attention—I don't want to repeat myself. The cottage closest to the river has significant structural damage. We don't know if it will remain standing or not. Those of you staying in that cottage, 'do not enter'. It's too dangerous. Also, the main entrance is off-limits. It's completely underwater. There is every possibility of sliding into the river if you go near it. We are responsible for your safety, so these rules are not negotiable. Those of you staying in the cottage will be redistributed to the other rooms."

"What about our belongings?" someone from the cottage asked.

"That should be the least of your concerns right now. It's a miracle you're alive and didn't get swept away by the floodwaters. Forget about your stuff. You are not going back to get it, and neither is anyone else. I'm sure others with access to their luggage will lend you spare clothes. Our contacts at headquarters have provided the authorities with your names and passport information. The Indian government will contact the embassies of your respective countries. This is being escalated to the highest levels."

Umbrella Lady's shrill voice rose above the murmur of the group.

"I bought special insurance! They'll evacuate me," she said. "Let me make a call, and I can have a helicopter here by the afternoon. Maybe I can even take a couple of you with me."

"No!" Marilyn replied. "I won't let you use our precious satellite phone minutes to save yourself and maybe two other people. It's great you have insurance that will send help for you, but no one leaves here on their own. I called the abbot of the order, and he insists we try to stay together as a group. Until we reach safety, we will remain as one. Understood?" Marilyn scanned the room to make sure everyone was listening.

Brahmachari Jeevan added, "We have enough rice and lentils to last a few more days. We will be serving the usual portion size for now, but please restrict yourself to one helping."

"For those of you not staying in the cottage, go to your rooms, pack up your belongings, and move up to the meditation hall," Marilyn ordered. "Cottage people—go directly to higher ground."

Len and I went back to our room. I didn't have much to pack. As we entered, we saw our roommates ripping the plastic off the mattresses.

"Hey! What are y'all doing?" Len confronted the men.

"Using the plastic to waterproof our luggage," one of them replied.

"You can't be serious. You couldn't even get your own bags across the bridge. Who do you think is going to carry all your stuff out of here?"

It was too late. All the mattresses had been ruthlessly skinned. Any more rain coming inside would soak right through. Thanks to Marilyn, our roommates were under the assumption an evacuation would happen that day, but I knew it would be impossible.

As we continued to pack, Len said, "You know, Niranjan, I'd been praying really hard that we'd have a Western-style toilet here at the ashram. Yeah, that prayer was big in my mind on the drive up here. But no such luck, huh?"

I chortled. "Do you practice yoga?" I asked.

"Yes, but what does that have to do with the toilet?"

"There's a posture called Malasana. It really helps when using an Indian style toilet. First, you squat with your feet together, then separate your thighs wider than your torso." I squatted to show him. "Next, lean forward so you're balanced, with your torso between your thighs. Then grab your shins with your hands, and hope you don't fall backwards into the hole. This posture relaxes your lower muscles and straightens the colon, so everything comes out in a straight shot."

"Huh," Len mused. "Yeah, that makes sense. I could never figure it out. I was too afraid I'd slip and fall. I tried the chair pose, but believe me, that didn't work out too well. I spoke to some of the other Westerners to see how they did it. You know what they told me?"

"What?"

"That they have Western-style toilets in their bathrooms! Ours is the only hole in the floor. They asked me why I didn't come over and use their bathroom. Well, how would I know? We were in silence! Ha!"

Len and I chuckled as we plodded through the mud back to the meditation hall. We passed Brahmachari Jeevan, who'd grasped the fabric of his dhoti below the waist to try and keep the edge from touching the soupy ground.

"You seem to be really knowledgeable about things," Len said. "Can I ask you something?"

"Sure," I replied.

"Why does Brama Chech—uh, Brama Cha-Cha…"

"You mean Brahmachari Jeevan?"

"Ugh, yes! I can't say his name. In my mind, I've been calling him BJ this whole time. Anyway, why does he always walk around grabbing his crotch?"

I burst out laughing. "Len, he's just trying to keep his white clothes from getting dirty. I promise, it's nothing weird. He's a celibate monk, after all."

I enjoyed Len's light-hearted company. It kept me from sinking into the uncertainty of our grave situation.

Chapter 15

Gone was the silent decorum of early morning. The meditation hall resembled an airport departure lounge filled with luggage and hopeful travellers. Some people were sitting casually on the floor, conversing loudly. Others were sprawled on their backs with their heads on their bags, succumbed to the weight of fatigue. Len was right—there had been a complete shift in energy. Listening to the buzz around me, all I heard was 'disaster', 'death' and 'destruction'. Marilyn and BJ were present but unable to control the volume or energy of the crowd.

Guru Ananda strode into the room, his normally smiling face aghast to see the change in behaviour. As soon as people noticed he was present, their legs crossed, their backs straightened, and the noise faded.

"I know our situation has changed," Ananda said, "and we are waiting for more updates. In the meantime, let's continue our meditations and try to keep the schedule as intended."

Marilyn interrupted, her normally strong voice feeble and shaky. "Um, excuse me. I have more information. It appears we are not the only area affected. The Shiva temple in Kedarnath, about forty miles away, is completely submerged in mud and water. No one knows how many have perished." She paused to collect herself. "We are waiting for further word from your various governments. I've been assured we are a high priority. The Indian authorities do not want an international incident with so many foreigners stranded in one place."

I wondered why Marilyn was still entertaining the expectation of being able to leave that day. Tens of thousands of devotees were on their way up to Gangotri—the birthplace of the river Ganges—at that time of year. All of them would be stranded as well. How many people had been driving when the storm was at its worst, with nowhere on the remote mountain roads to take shelter? My heart grieved as I wondered how many landslides had buried travellers and villagers. How many people were stranded out in the open— on the roads and highways—without food, water, and safe shelter? It was logical for those people to be higher priorities for rescue.

Desperate voices began to sound around the room.

"I can contact my congressmen! They'll escalate this to the State Department."

"We should start a social media campaign to raise awareness of our situation."

"Why won't you let us call our travel insurance companies?"

Hal, who was beside me, looked to me to tell him what was happening. We slipped outside, away from the noise, where I could focus on what I had to tell him. There was so much to convey. It was too much to write down, but being able to speak meant he could read my lips. I summarised Guru Ananda's message from the morning, along with the news from Marilyn.

Len joined us outside.

"My goodness," he said. "There's so much fear and negativity there. I can't be around it anymore. I need to go somewhere else. Away from the ashram. Do you want to come with me?"

"What?" I said. "Len, the river is in spate, and we could get more rain. We're surrounded by unstable mountains and have no idea which direction to head to get help. I know it's unpleasant to hear everyone freaking out, but it's much safer to stay here for now. Let's just wait and see what happens." Hal and I went back inside. Reluctantly, Len followed.

Guru Ananda posed a question to the group.

"In case, we cannot get everyone out of here at once, how many want to leave immediately, and how many are willing to stay longer? Let's make a list of those who want to be the first to go."

Several hands shot up, and a few more extended hesitantly.

Len leaned over to me and whispered, "We should let the most fearful people leave first."

"I agree." I pushed my own fear deeper within me.

Our teacher tried his best to lead the group back into meditation, but no one was feeling it. It was past ten in the morning, and Marilyn wasn't helping matters by scuttering in and out constantly. Presumably, she was leaving to make calls or check messages. So far, I hadn't seen any sign of the phone. She was wise to keep it out of sight. If anyone saw it, I expected nothing less than a second mini-rebellion—a battle for the satellite communications device.

The next time she entered the building, she was confronted by several group members.

"Please stop asking me to call your insurance companies!" she replied to their many pleas. "There will be no individual evacuations. We will coordinate this as a group."

By that point, Guru Ananda had given up and left the hall, telling Marilyn he'd be in his room. She was fully in charge, her stress level through the roof and rapidly approaching orbit. I could only imagine what was going through her mind. BJ was by her side, as always, but seemed clueless as to how to help.

Len stood up and looked at me. "I don't think this is going anywhere. Let's go back to our room. If a helicopter comes for us, we'll hear it from there."

I followed him out. We went back to the annex and stretched out on the mattresses.

"What do you do in Dallas?" I asked.

"I'm the minister at a spiritual living centre. I teach self-love through conscious living. And what I see happening there"—he pointed towards the meditation hall—"is neither self-love nor conscious living. Fear is taking control, and Marilyn isn't helping matters. I would be handling this very differently if I were in charge."

"I saw you rolling those prayer beads yesterday," I said. "What mantra were you chanting?"

"I make up my own. I do three to five thousand a day. Yesterday morning, sitting in meditation, my legs and back were killing me. To take my mind off the pain, I repeated positive affirmations."

"Like what?"

"I am an active, virile, twenty-five-year-old athlete, blessed with abundance."

"Huh. You don't say."

"Yeah. I seed my subconscious mind with the type of body and life I want for myself, and it simply manifests itself."

It was a new concept to me. Creating an affirmation of one's choosing and reciting it thousands of times. Although I didn't fully buy into his methodology, something was definitely working for Len. He was in his mid-sixties, yet his stride still held an energetic bounce. His curiosity and enthusiasm were apparent, his positive outlook contagious. He was also supremely confident. Fearless, even.

"Last night," he said, "I repeated to myself one thousand times that we'll be rescued and no harm will come to us. So we'll be fine."

Len picked up his book and began to read. As I lay on my side, I could see the page he was reading. Almost every word was highlighted or underlined. Notes crowded the margins.

"A well-worn book. What's it about?" I asked.

"It's a scientific approach to understanding the mind. I like to examine different schools of thought, various religions. Then I mix together the best ideas from each and create my own blend of spirituality."

"Have you always been a minister?"

"My parents put me in the seminary at age sixteen, but I was kicked out a year later. Apparently, I asked too many questions."

The twinkle in his eye told me his rebellious streak was still alive and well.

"After that," he continued, "I went to college, entered the business world, climbed up the corporate ladder, yada yada—that whole deal. When I was fifty-five, I was diagnosed with a brain tumour. The doctor wanted to perform surgery. I refused. I changed my diet, became a vegan, and started my affirmations. I went back a year later, and the tumour was gone. The doctors couldn't believe it. I decided to quit my job and go back to school to become a minister. Now I have my own church and my own following. It's a good gig."

"Maybe we could do some affirmations together—after I get some sleep," I said.

"Sure, anytime."

I woke up as people began to trickle into the dining hall for lunch. I hurried to join them, hoping to be apprised of the current situation. I sat with Jacques and asked if there was any news, but he had nothing to report. He was beside himself with frustration. His trip was ruined, and he was extremely unhappy about it. I tried to cheer him up by reciting a positive affirmation inspired by Len, but he was too cranky to listen. I could tell from the mood in the dining hall that, even though we had only completed a day and a half of our retreat, people were excited about the prospect of leaving.

Marilyn didn't make any further announcements. I doubted any sort of rescue attempt would happen within the next few days, but at least the authorities knew our location. The rest of the afternoon was designated as free time. Some people went back to the meditation hall, others to rest in their rooms. Guru Ananda remained out of sight.

My goal for the afternoon was to eliminate the rest of my sleep debt. The last thing I needed was to fall sick from the stress of fatigue. Len also chose to rest. I noticed our roommates had returned the plastic to their mattresses. Reality was settling in.

Chapter 16

Len and I missed teatime. It was dusk by the time we woke up, and the regular crowd was beginning to gather for dinner. Several people sat on the floor, heads in hands, looking defeated. I wondered if we'd missed an important briefing. We were served a simple meal of steamed rice with lentils— strictly one portion for each of us. The serving seemed smaller than normal. A twinge of fear stirred in my gut as I realised the food was already being rationed carefully. The group leaders must have been notified of some troubling new information. I chewed each grain of rice well, tamping my worry a bit with each swallow. I filled the rest of my stomach with water in an attempt to satisfy my appetite.

Marilyn materialised, looking frazzled.

"I have updates," she said. "Please listen carefully. More rain is forecast. We haven't been able to reach anyone else in the government through our contacts. They are extremely busy. This entire region of the country is in a state of emergency." She took in a sharp breath. Her eyes filled with tears that crested and fell with the next wave of bad news. "Hundreds of people have lost their lives in the flooding. Thousands more are missing, presumed dead. Hundreds of thousands are stranded without necessities. I don't know how long it will be until help can come for us. We have enough food to last a few days, so…" Her voice trailed off. She took a moment to gather her thoughts. "Um, okay. The generator is waterlogged and not working, so we have no power. In the morning, we'll need some volunteers to try and collect wood for cooking."

"The program tomorrow will be different. Guru Ananda understands the anxiety and fear people are struggling with under these circumstances, but we also came here with a commitment to better ourselves. So we will have a short meditation session at five a.m. Helga has volunteered to lead the group through a yoga class afterward, then there will be one more short meditation. After breakfast, the schedule will be left open so we can focus on getting more information about our evacuation plans."

"Tonight, you will take turns sitting on the balcony upstairs so we can keep watch for bad weather. Brahmachari Jeevan will pass around a sheet for people to sign up in pairs for shifts from nine p.m. until five a.m. Any questions?"

By the time the signup sheet made its way to Len and me, the only remaining shift was at 1:00 a.m. Len scribbled our names down. The sun was setting, the last bit of daylight turning swiftly into darkness. The only light inside the building came from the swinging flashlights people carried while moving from one place to another.

Len and I decided to sneak down to the river to see what the water was doing. I put on my headlamp, and he grabbed his flashlight. A few stars were visible through the thinning cloud cover. The crescent of the waxing moon came into view now and then, little bits of moonlight setting the whitecaps aglow. To our disappointment, the river gave no indication of receding.

"If death were standing before us, what would you do?" I asked Len.

"I would ask it to go away because I'm not ready to die."

"And if it didn't listen?"

"I would outrun it! After all, I have the body of a virile twenty-five-year-old athlete."

Len sounded serious. Maybe for him, it would be possible.

"What about you?" he asked. "What would you do?"

"I need to get home to my family, so dying isn't an option for me right now."

I tried to make it sound like a joke, but truth was, our life-or-death scenario really had me feeling paralysed. How would we get out of there? And when?

I asked Len to make an affirmation for me to repeat.

"How about this one?" he said. "I know the divine wisdom within me guides and directs our every thought, word, and action to bring us back safely to our respective homes. Divine wisdom now safely guides us on our journey."

Together, we made several rowdy proclamations to the sky, the river, the mountains, the weather gods. I must admit, it felt good to yell. I drew in several deep breaths of fresh mountain air.

Emboldened by Len's supreme confidence in the face of death, I made my own proclamation.

"Let it be known, Death, whenever you come for me, I will greet you with strength! I will have no fear! No regrets! I will continue my path in the next life!" For good measure, I stood tall and puffed out my chest. I vowed we would all make it out safely.

We sat for a while, listening to the strength of the river. The silhouette of the surrounding mountains added a mystical feel to the air. I considered how my complex karmic web had somehow joined Len's on the side of the mountain, thousands of miles from home. He was outgoing and extroverted; I was reflective and introverted. He liked to crack jokes; I could be a little too serious. There was even a generational gap between the two of us. He was old enough to be my father, yet young at heart. He truly felt like a long-lost brother.

I squinted at the weather watching balcony. I could barely make out two heads poking above the railing.

"I wonder who's up there right now," I said. "Maybe we should offer to take over their shift. They might be tired, but I'm wide awake."

"Me too," Len said. "I'm energised. Fired up. Let's do it."

"Maybe we can come up with a plan to get out of here. I know Marilyn is trying to make arrangements, but she has no clue how things work in India. And imagine the logistics involved in scheduling tens of thousands—maybe hundreds of thousands—of rescues. A promise in a phone conversation is one thing, but the reality is we could be waiting weeks for someone to come help us out of here. If we get lucky, the government might be able to organise a food drop. But I'm not sure I want to wait around and see if they come through in time. We need to have a plan from our end in case no one comes."

Making our way upstairs to the balcony, we carefully tiptoed past the weary souls asleep on the floor. The Puerto Rican twins were on duty, their eyes glued to the river. They were crouched with their arms tightly wrapped around each other, craning their necks to see as far upstream as they could. In their minds, the rain was on its way back, and the river could rise higher at any moment. In my mind, I saw nature resting after a colossal outburst. The twins were thankful to pass responsibility to Len and me. My hunch had been right; they were exhausted. We sat down, our legs stretched out, backs against the wall. The sky did not reveal any imminent threats.

"Why did you come on this trip?" Len asked.

"To get away from work."

"Ha! Go on."

I explained some of the problems I was having with my medical practice.

"I knew it would be a lot to keep track of when I started out, but I'm at the point where I feel like I'm drowning. I've been so successful that I can't handle the patient load. I know it's a good problem to have, but I find it impossible to turn away new patients, so my schedule is perpetually overbooked. And I hate to keep people waiting, so my eye is on the clock all day long. I barely have a second to catch my breath between patients."

"Why don't you just say no to taking on new patients?" Len asked. "You're the one in charge."

"Honestly, I don't know how to say no. When someone asks something of me, I feel obligated to say yes."

"That's your problem right there, my brother. Why do you think that is?"

I sat quietly for a moment. I had the answer to his question, but I wasn't sure I wanted to talk about it.

"I can hear the wheels turning in your head, Niranjan," Len said. "Tell me."

His invitation to share was like someone opening my rusty sluice gates. It all came spilling out. I explained that growing up, I lived in a house with my grandfather and fourteen other family members. My grandfather—though I loved him dearly—was someone the entire family feared. He had a vicious temper. It was his way or nothing.

Every morning, he'd wake me up early and have me clean his car before I went to school. We'd sit down for breakfast, and he'd feed me balls of rice dipped in clarified butter. I hated it, but I dared not say anything. Every morning I would choke it down without complaint. After school, I'd walk to his clinic and sit in the waiting room for hours until he was done for the day. I remember a few times I became so bored, I snuck into the exam room between patients and hid in one of the cabinets so I could hear what he was doing.

I didn't enjoy the time I spent with my grandfather, but I craved his approval. I also needed his protection. He was the alpha dog of the house, and most of the other kids living there picked on me constantly. They teased me, locked me in closets, did things to get in trouble, then blamed them on me. I figured if I spent all my time with my grandfather, they couldn't bother me as much.

Len nodded in understanding as I spoke, which encouraged me to continue.

"I became a doctor and moved to America because that's what he decided for me. During my medical residency years, I would say yes to everything—overtime work, research projects, all of it. I put in over one hundred hours a week, with very little sleep. Looking back at it, I know it was way too much. But at the end of it all, I landed a fellowship at Harvard Medical School. So in that respect, it paid off."

"Yes," said Len. "It paid off, but at what cost to your physical and emotional health? Have you explored saying no lately? Maybe try it with one person and see how it feels. Your wife must see you working so hard. What does she think of all of this?"

"She constantly encourages me to say no—to set boundaries for the sake of my own sanity. I just can't seem to do it."

"She sounds very wise."

"Oh, she's a true angel. My best friend and the most steadfast supporter of all my big dreams and crazy ideas. I'd be lost without her. You know what? She called her mom after our first date to say she'd met her future husband. I'm a little slower, so it took me until our third date to realise I wanted to spend the rest of my life with her. We were engaged two weeks later and married two months after that."

Len and I were so engrossed in our conversation that we completely forgot about watching the river. Hours passed while we talked. By the time we remembered to pay attention to the weather, the sky was completely clear. Billions of stars hung silently above us. I could even see the Milky Way galaxy, illuminated like a thin veil in the sky. Everything was completely still. And suddenly, I felt microscopic. Insignificant.

It reminded me of when I was a boy and would go outside at night when everyone else in the house was taking up too much space—making too much noise. There was very little light pollution in Bangalore at that time, and I was quite fond of staring into the night sky. The stars were easily visible, and I loved to search for the constellations hidden among them. I would reach out to the night and imagine scooping the tiny lights into the palm of my hand.

I remember one time I tried to figure the distance of one light-year in relation to the distance I could jump by crouching low to the ground and launching forward with all my might. It was comparatively minute, of course. A jump too small for even God to see. The idea of an infinite universe was a mindboggling concept at that age, but the finite limits of my own physical body were quite apparent to me. Eventually, though, I began to feel an unsettling awareness of being something more than just my body alone. Obviously, my brain was part of my body, but perhaps my mind was more than the sum of my body's parts—something beyond the input of my five senses. I remember wondering, *What would it be like to be someone else? If I wasn't standing here, where would I be? Who, exactly, is the person asking this question? Where do I find comfort if I feel uneasy in my own body?*

Chapter 17

As promised, Helga was waiting for everyone to assemble for the 5:00 a.m. yoga class. A German woman in her fifties, she had a sunny smile and kind blue eyes. Her bleached hair was tied up in a neat bun secured by a silky white bow. Thin-framed glasses made her look stylish. She would've fit right in with the groups of Westerners we saw in Haridwar.

Helga began the class with grounding postures—appropriate since I didn't think anyone was feeling grounded in light of what was happening. The yoga turned out to be a welcome distraction; I found it easier for my mind to remain quiet while my body was moving. Slowly stretching my muscles was very relaxing for me. Stretching my mind was another matter. One thing I'd learned from the retreat was that sitting still in meditation was surprisingly taxing. An hour was my upper limit. Any longer, and I turned into a concoction of aching body parts and throbbing frustration. Knowing the schedule was abbreviated, I was practically giddy with relief. I had no idea how I would've managed eleven more days of it all. I clearly wasn't ready for such a robust spiritual commitment.

BJ joined the class late and snuck to the back near Len and me. I watched him suspiciously out of the corner of my eye. He appeared to be executing his own routine, moving completely counter to what we were doing. When Helga asked us to stand, he would sit. When we sat, he would jump up and grab his back as if in pain. I'd spied him walking earlier with his usual no-nonsense gait, and the quick way he carried himself didn't indicate he had back problems. Why would he feign an injury? I surmised he wanted to escape the rigorous rituals and meditations often prescribed for apprentice monks such as himself. He was staying in Guru Ananda's room, which meant he was under the watchful eye of his teacher for much of the day. That must have been his only available moment to rebel. For the second half of class, he showed very little interest, only jiggling one leg or the other on occasion to keep up appearances. Perhaps he, too, was rethinking his recent life choices.

At exactly 6:00 a.m., Guru Ananda took the wheel of the class from Helga and steered us straight into the truth of the situation. "What we face right now is a perfect test for you to keep your mind and body aligned. Your mind wants to wander back home, but your body is trapped on this little piece of land between the mountains and the river. There will be no easy way out. Yes, we have cheated death so far, but each new day may present a different challenge."

"Personally, I am ready to die at any time. Even now, at this moment, I am ready. But every minute I am alive, I am here to serve you by supporting your spiritual practice. I am just one pillar. Each one of you is a pillar. Together, we can hold up the world if we must, but it cannot be done alone. It can only be done when there is togetherness. I sense everyone is now on their own journey, not physically, but mentally. Many of you want to get out of here as quickly as possible.

But again, don't waste this precious opportunity. Very few get the chance to experience such a test."

"Maintaining the body and mind as one is challenging, yes. Your body is seated here, but in a second, your mind can travel to a distant part of the planet. We must find a way to anchor it here, with the body, in the present moment. That is mindfulness. We can use our focus on the breath as a rope to tether the mind to the body. Ignoring the mind's call to wander may be tedious at first, but it becomes easier whenever there is mindfulness."

Before we could leave for breakfast, Marilyn made an announcement. "After we eat, you'll have the morning to yourselves. There will be no more meditation today. We're not certain if—"

The distant *thwhip, thwhip, thwhip* of a helicopter echoed across the sky, rapidly increasing in volume. Len and I stared at each other, taking a second to process the sound. We all jumped up and ran outside as it flew out of sight over the mountain.

"They didn't see us," Jacques said in a panic.

"At least, there's rescue activity in the area. That's a good sign, right?" I said, trying to sound encouraging. "Did you get a look at the helicopter? How big was it?"

"Quite big. And green. Like the Army, yes?" Jacques replied.

"Yes! That means the Indian military has been mobilised. This is great news!"

"Okay, yes. Good news. I agree. We will be okay?"

"Yes, we'll be okay."

"Wait," said Jacques, looking around. "They cannot land here."

"They can't. They would have to hover and lower a line or something."

"Can they do that? It's quite windy here."

"I don't know."

I knew I needed to go back up the mountain, farther that time, and find a spot where rescue could get to us more easily.

Breakfast consisted of flattened rice flakes and plain black tea. No milk. I figured they sourced it from the villagers I'd met on my first day there. The villagers. I suddenly had an overwhelming urge to go check on them. I knew Marilyn wouldn't let me leave, and BJ had been going around at random times, taking a headcount. I couldn't be found missing—that would cause all kinds of trouble. I had no choice but to go to the top dog, Guru Ananda. I resolved to find him.

Outside, people were getting creative with their free time. Several group members had each contributed an item of white clothing and were intently stitching together a giant white flag. They'd sharpened a twig to make holes in the cloth and were using brown string from an old burlap rice sack to patchwork it all together. Someone found a log that had been ejected by the river and fashioned it into a crude flagpole. After a bit of hard work, the flag was raised, and the world's newest micronation came into existence. How fitting that it flew a dirty, droopy white flag of surrender. I hoped it would convey our desperation to anyone flying overhead.

Guru Ananda was sitting outside his room watching all the morning's action with amusement. I'd just mustered up the courage to approach him when Len came jogging up to me.

"Hey, Niranjan, I have a great idea," he said. "You wanna help?"

I was anxious to secure permission to go see the villagers, but I couldn't say no to Len. "Sure. What are you thinking?" I asked.

"You'll see. Follow me."

He led me to a little garden that had been flattened by the storm. It was bordered by bright white bricks that were so clean from the rain they looked like they'd been freshly painted. I understood immediately what he wanted to do. We made many trips back and forth to a sandy area near the riverbank. Intent on our task, we laid the bricks down, one by one, to create a large SOS sign.

Chapter 18

Guru Ananda was sitting serenely, appreciating a tree while listening to the clipped, metallic notes of a warbler. It was late morning by the time I approached him, and he was flanked by the two people I was trying to avoid. BJ was unrolling a small solar panel while Marilyn was on the phone. Again. I was beginning to wonder if she'd lied to us about having a limited number of minutes available to contact help. I had no idea who she was talking to or what was being said, but every time the phone rang, her eyebrows dug a deep furrow. By the time she hung up, they would be back in place. Clearly, someone was making promises to allay her fears, but I wondered if she was making any real progress on a rescue plan.

When she saw me approaching, she waved her hand to shoo me away, but I ignored her. I was determined to check on the villagers.

My guru afforded me a gracious welcome. "Come, doctor, have a seat."

"Thank you." I took a deep breath, ready to make my case. "I—"

"We could use your skills," he said, his brown eyes showing concern. "The village uphill supplied us with milk and fresh vegetables. They would not accept money in exchange. Such kind people. Would you mind going to see if they need any medical assistance? I thought of asking you as soon as the flood happened. Anyhow, I'm glad you're here now. Please, go and do what you can."

Marilyn had one ear on our conversation. She abruptly hung up and interjected, "There's another doctor in the group. His name is… I forget."

She looked at BJ, who consulted his clipboard and said, "Jim. The homeopathic doctor."

"Yes, that's him. Can you take him along?"

"Sure," I replied. I scanned the group to see if he was outside. I spotted him immediately. He was tall and gangly, with an oversized T-shirt hanging loosely from his wiry frame. His long brown hair was pulled back into a low ponytail.

"Jim!" I shouted and waved him over. He immediately ran towards us, a wide grin revealing his perfect teeth.

"Can you go with Dr Seshadri to check on the villagers?" Marilyn asked.

"Absolutely. I'd be happy to." Jim hurried to his room and quickly returned with his medical bag. It looked like the one my grandfather used to carry: leather with a split handle that opened at the top. It reminded me of the days I used to accompany him on house calls. He always dressed in a tailored three-piece suit, even for emergencies in the middle of the night. I would follow him into the patients' homes, carrying his bag. I was his faithful assistant even though I was barely twelve at the time. I wondered what he would think of me there, in my wrinkled blue scrub bottoms and dirty white T-shirt.

Jim and I set out for the village right away. My previous hike made me the default expert on the terrain, so I was the guide. Jim followed close behind me, rattling off the names of his homeopathic remedies in rapid-fire succession. "Arnica for bruising, Apis for insect bites and stings, Rhus tox for arthritis…"

I listened half-heartedly while taking stock of our surroundings. Even though I'd gone that way a couple of days before, it was unrecognisable. Slushy clods of earth buried the trail, muddying the direction we were to walk. Uprooted trees were strewn about, creating multiple blockades. Having no apparent path, we could only head in the general direction of the village. I kept the river in sight as a guide and didn't let on that I was uncertain about our exact route. Our progress was aggravatingly slow. Every step was slippery, and Jim stopped every few seconds. Not necessarily from difficulty walking, but to examine, with great interest, what was left of the ground cover. *Was he also an herbologist?* I wondered. Due to my red-green colour blindness, all of the plants looked the same to me. I preferred to stare at the vibrant blue mountains in the distance, which I did while Jim was lost in his own little world of flora.

"Jim, we ought to hurry up a bit," I finally said. I wanted to spend as much time as possible at the village. Besides, without a designated trail to follow, it could take us a while to find our way back. It required a combination of strength, balance, and endurance to push our way through the aftermath of the storm. Each step forward spoke to the fragility of life in the face of a natural disaster. I was thankful to have Jim for company. Unlike my previous hike in solitude, I no longer wanted to be alone.

We were stopped in our tracks by a trench, freshly carved out of the mountainside by excessive runoff. The new geographical feature was steep, deep, and slick. The span across was maybe eight feet. Even if we could somehow jump, there was no way to tell if the ground on the other side would accept a two-hundred-pound body flying through the air. It wasn't a question of who should go first. It was obvious we should turn back and head to the safety of the retreat centre. I felt defeated—I had hoped that would be our path to rescue.

"Wait a minute," Jim said, looking around. "Maybe we can make a bridge." I wasn't on board with the dangerous workaround, but Jim was already off in the woods searching for materials we could use. He returned after a few minutes, dragging a long log behind him. "There are a ton of smaller downed trees around here. I really think this might work."

We carried the log to the edge of the trench, held it upright, and then let it fall across the gap. The other end crashed to the ground on the opposite side. We found a few more logs of varying lengths and diameters, placing them side by side across the gap. The plan was to run across them faster than they could roll out from under our feet.

Jim threw down the gauntlet by flinging his medicine bag across to the other side. There was no turning back. Well, at least for Jim. I had no doubt he would make the crossing, even if only to retrieve his medicines. The man hardly hesitated. Logs bounced under his feet as he sprinted across, but they didn't roll, and the ground on either side held firm.

I was reassured but still worried—I weighed a bit more than Jim. I tried to channel some of my childhood fearlessness and prepared to make a run for it. After all, I used to climb to the highest branches of the giant mango tree in our yard. I even chased monkeys from my branch so I could pluck the choicest mangoes. The monkeys would bounce from one tree to another, sling-shotting themselves with their prehensile tails. My brother and I would try to imitate them by jumping from the tree to the roof. The margin for error was non-existent, yet I had still done it.

Where had that bravery gone? I jogged in place for a few seconds, blowing several breaths into my cupped hands. I let out a loud 'Aiyaaaah!' as I ran across, collapsing to the ground on the other side as if I had just crossed the finish line of a marathon. My shirt was covered in mud, yes, but my body was still in one piece. I was feeling good. Jim and I scrambled on all fours up a steep incline and pulled ourselves onto a ledge that connected back with the main trail.

I froze. I knew exactly where we were. The remnants of the village were ahead—a few standing walls with holes where the windows and doors had been. The roofs were gone. No one was there. Only two days before, there were women working, children playing… I stumbled along, hoping to find some sign of life. The terraced field where I had encountered the old woman was gone. In its place was a steep drop-off where the crops once stood. There were no animals in sight, either.

I was beside myself. How could they have survived? I described to Jim what the village had been like before. We were shaken by what we saw and agreed to continue on. I prayed the villagers had been able to move somewhere safer. I had my camera with me but had no interest in taking pictures. I didn't want any physical reminders of how I felt at that moment.

I led Jim to the scenic area where the large rock jutted out of the mountain. From there, I could see exactly how we had survived the storm. The narrow valley upstream from the retreat caused the water level in the river to rise very quickly during the storm. The village and crop fields took a direct hit, which triggered a massive landslide. The tons of earth that tore down the side of the mountain shifted the course of the river, pushing it away from the ashram. If that hadn't happened, the river would have immersed us. We would've drowned in our rooms that night. I was working it out in my head and didn't discuss it with Jim. He didn't pick up on the change in scenery, as it was his first time there. He hadn't seen the way things were before.

I felt more confident as we continued on. The ground was wet but less slippery, and the trail was well-defined. The little temple farther up the path was completely intact; Varahi was unmoved by the destruction that radiated from her in all directions. I sat for a few minutes, offering prayers of gratitude on behalf of all the survivors at the ashram. I also prayed for the villagers who may or may not have made it out alive.

Just past the shrine, the trail made a sharp left turn. That was where I turned back on the first day. We forged ahead with ample daylight left. All I heard were our footsteps. Jim had a more efficient stride; I was dragging my left foot. Sitting cross-legged for such long periods the previous couple of days had inflamed my sciatic nerve. Going uphill put a strain on my iliopsoas muscle. I tried to compensate for the discomfort by hunching over as I moved.

"You know, I used to be a cross-country runner. I've had my share of troubles with the iliopsoas muscle," Jim revealed. "I can help you with that."

"Really? That would be amazing. It's getting so bad I can barely walk. I think it's in spasm."

"Lie down flat on your stomach." He completed a few manoeuvres on my leg that sent excruciating pain shooting from my injured hip. As soon as he finished, though, I felt better. I couldn't tell if it was because the pain he'd inflicted on me had stopped, or he had actually reset the offending tendons and ligaments. Either way, it worked. I wondered what other skills he possessed. "Here, use this to support yourself." Jim handed me a tree branch that resembled a cane.

We must have gone up a dozen switchbacks, each turn taking us higher. We passed two cows perched precariously on a steep slope. Their jowls twirled rhythmically as they munched on leaves, oblivious to any dangers of falling off the mountain. I envied them. They had no choice but to be mindful. They were blessed with the inability to fear what may or may not happen in the future. I hoped the presence of the cows meant people were nearby. The thought gave me a burst of fresh energy. Maybe the villagers were safe after all.

I had read stories about the Indian Ocean tsunami in 2004. Hours before it hit, the indigenous tribes living in coastal areas of the Andaman and Nicobar Islands followed animals to higher ground, and they survived while others perished. They didn't need seismic data or advanced warning systems to tell them it was coming. Those in tune with their ancestral lands often implement survival measures gleaned from past generations. Perhaps the locals in the area were able to do something similar.

We had been walking for hours. I was starting to worry we might have to turn back without any helpful information about the fate of the villagers or our potential rescue. But around the next bend, the path straightened out and led directly to a walled compound. It looked out of place amid the dense trees. I heard voices, and Jim and I rushed to the open gap where a gate once stood. The villagers were there, safe. Children were making games in the dirt; cows were tied up in a corner. Half a dozen men quietly squatted on the floor of the portico, and the women were conversing with each other in strained tones.

The sight of Jim and me caught their attention. They stared in shock. After a brief pause, their surprise gave way to a burst of energy, and they ran to us as if we were there to rescue them. We hardly looked the part. I hadn't shaved for days and was dishevelled and dirty from all my mishaps on the way up. Jim had no idea what they were saying to him. I had to translate for both parties.

One man appeared, exclaiming in rapid Hindi, "You are a gift from the heavens! We survived a major flood. Our ancestors always warned us about upsetting the mountains. The people down in the flat land have no respect for this sacred place. They cut trees and build dams, guest houses, resorts—"

A woman joined in, saying, "I have never heard such loud thunder as I did that night! I have never seen the rain come down with such anger! In the middle of the night, the river came close and made such big noises. We left everything and barely made it here for shelter."

"This used to be an old government guest house," the man explained. "They turned it into a school for the local children. Now it is the only thing we have. Everything else is gone. Can you help us?"

"I hope I can help," I said. "I'm a doctor. Is anyone injured or sick?"

"Yes, the man on the cot. We keep him separate from the rest. He has TB."

Jim jumped back in astonishment. He obviously knew how contagious tuberculosis could be. The best the villagers could do to isolate the old man from others was to place him outside so the droplets from his lungs might be carried away by the wind before infecting anyone else.

Blankets covered his lower half while his torso was exposed to the elements. His body was completely emaciated, with hard knots of bone protruding under his thin, wizened skin. Sweat covered his chest, which heaved in an unhealthy pattern. I recognised the Cheyne-Stokes breathing, which portends imminent death. I had worked in a TB sanatorium as part of my medical internship in India and had seen far too many manifestations of the horrific illness.

I rolled up my left sleeve and pointed to a raised, pigmented vaccination mark. "Jim, it's okay, I have immunity against TB. I'll examine this man. Maybe someone here speaks English. Why don't you ask the others if they need any of your medicines for arthritis and such?"

The men, women, and children gathered around Jim as he pointed to his knees and shoulders. It looked like he was playing a game of charades, and the kids began to mimic his movements, laughing. It was highly entertaining to them. The men and women just looked confused. I intervened with my broken Hindi, telling them his bag contained remedies. Immediately, two of the men ran inside the building and came out with a bag of various pills. They were all still sealed in blister packs. The man who was holding the bag brought it closer to Jim and shoved it in his hands. I took the transparent plastic bag and found aspirin, fever-reducing medicines, a handful of painkillers, and TB meds. Clearly, there was a doctor somewhere nearby who had provided them.

"Where did you get these?" I asked the men.

"We work near Uttarkashi at one of the rest houses that serve pilgrims. There is a mobile clinic that comes there once a week. They give us these medicines. Some of them are old. None of them have instructions."

"Do you give the old man these medicines?"

"We want to, but we don't understand how many to give him and how often."

"Has he been to a hospital?"

"Yes, we took him to a district hospital. They kept him there for a few weeks and said there is nothing more they could do for him, so he is now with us."

Sadly, his disease had progressed far beyond any pills or advice I could offer. The only things that could help him were comfort measures. I took his skeletal hand in mine. He had no teeth. His cheeks were deeply sunken, his eyes barely open. I stroked his head with my other hand. A woman who looked like she might be his daughter burst into tears.

"I'm sorry," I said.

She understood there was nothing to be done.

"We are visiting the ashram down by the river. Do you need any supplies?" I asked.

"Our food is gone," answered a thin, middle-aged woman.

"I can arrange to give you some."

"Thank you, sir, thank you. I will send my son and nephew with you to get it."

I had not asked anyone at the retreat centre if we had extra rice or lentils to share with the people. I already knew the answer. But there were children there. I wouldn't be able to sleep if I knew they were going hungry.

Jim was examining a woman with a swollen elbow that looked like it could be gout. He prescribed a couple of different homeopathic preparations. He didn't have spare bottles with him, so she tore an old newspaper, folded it into a packet, and accepted a spoonful of the tiny white balls. She had likely never seen such pills and treated them with reverence.

It was late afternoon, and we would soon be losing daylight. Jim and I bid farewell to the villagers and started back down the mountain with two men responsible for bringing the food back.

The short young man who led us was energetic and talkative. "Where are you from?" he asked me in Hindi.

"I'm from America, but I grew up in South India. It's my first time in this part of the country."

He began to speak in broken English. "America! Big country, so nice people. I guide the tourists for trekking. Good guide. I take you places."

Jim's ears perked up. He could finally converse with a local in his own language. "I'm Jim. What's your name?"

"Name is Ram."

"Thank you for coming with us," I said. "It was hard to get up here."

Ram switched back to Hindi. "No problem, sir. I know a better way back. You are down by the river?" Ram pointed in the opposite direction. Or maybe it wasn't the opposite direction. I knew I was a little turned around at that point. I broke back into Hindi to better explain to him. I didn't want to end up in the wrong place and have to backtrack. We'd been out all day, and I was afraid we wouldn't make it before dark. Marilyn would freak out if we didn't get back by then, and I might too. We didn't even have our flashlights with us. I knew the thick forest canopy would plunge everything into darkness once the sun set.

"Yes, I know your place. Tapovana," Ram reassured us. The trail he led us on went down the other side of the mountain, away from the river. There was dense foliage, and it was better maintained. The gradient was also a little less steep. With Ram leading the way, I let my guard down and began to check out the scenery. I was no longer Jim's guide, just a tourist led by a local. I felt relieved I was not responsible for taking us both back.

I stepped on a rock that seemed safely secured in the dirt, but it gave way, clacking and bouncing down the mountainside. My right foot slipped off the trail, determined to follow it. *Shit!* Instinctively, I reached out for a tree branch to regain my balance, but it snapped in my hand. I completely lost my balance and started to fall in the direction of death. Ram spun around and grabbed my arm with his strong hands while using some sort of superhuman powers to keep his feet planted on the narrow path. I pulled my free arm around, grabbed on to his muscular forearm, and hauled myself back to safety.

"Careful, sir," he said with a head bobble. "The ground is very slippery. Do not catch hold of the tree parts. They might not hold you. Please follow attentively."

Jim was shaken by the incident and slowed down considerably. Every step was measured and cautious. Dusk was fading to darkness as we set foot on the ashram grounds. Ram had brought us back through an entirely different route. He was a local map—a walking GPS. I couldn't wait to introduce him to Guru Ananda, but there was no one to be seen. Perhaps they were in the meditation hall.

The faint aroma of freshly steamed rice told me the kitchen was open. I snuck into the small storeroom off the dining area. I grabbed a twenty-pound bag of rice and a couple ten-pound bags of lentils. The pantry was nearly empty. Guilt and fear washed over me as I carried half of our remaining sustenance outside to the waiting men.

Ram and his cousin gratefully accepted the stolen gifts. They placed the bags on their shoulders and ran off into the night. They disappeared into the forest with no light, no shoes, and an extra forty pounds of weight. Incredible.

Ram was the name of the Hindu god who journeyed thousands of miles from northern India to its southern tip, building a bridge to Sri Lanka in order to rescue his kidnapped wife, Sita. The Ram I met that day seemed capable of similar feats. I was certain, given the opportunity, he would lead us all to safety. I didn't know how I would be able to convince Marilyn of the idea. Perhaps she'd be willing to go along with it once she discovered we only had three days of food left.

Chapter 19

A booming voice emanated from the meditation hall. It was Len. He was leading the evening prayer in his own unique form. Everyone in the group was seated in a circle holding hands, including Guru Ananda and Marilyn. No one was above or below another. When Len spoke, he exuded confidence. His voice was animated, his words convincing. It was a spontaneous outpouring of feeling.

"I know there is One Power. One Presence. I know It is infinite and all-knowing. I know It has always been, and always will be. It is the seen and the unseen, the known and the unknown. Everything is created out of It because It is all there is."

"I know this Infinite Presence is within me and within you and is the same Creative Principle that exists in the essence of all people. I know each of us is one with the only Mind that there is; therefore, we are one with all life. I embody my connection—and the connection of everybody here—with that Infinite Intelligence that I know to be God."

"I now declare that each one of you here is guided and protected by the Infinite Intelligence. I know that the strength of this Infinite Presence fills each one of us and will allow us to make a journey to safety with ease and grace. Having made this declaration, I now give thanks to the power of the Infinite. Together we affirm this truth as we say: And so it is."

"And so it is," repeated a handful of participants.

Guru Ananda chuckled. Some of the Westerners grumbled as if that type of prayer hadn't been exotic enough for them. Marilyn was looking cross-eyed at Len. He was in her bad books. By association, I was sure I'd be too. I decided it wasn't a good time to talk with Marilyn and Guru Ananda. I needed Len's wise counsel before I could approach the leaders with my idea for escape.

The portion size at dinnertime was a scoop of rice and lentils. Someone would figure out soon enough that rations had gone missing, and our portions would likely shrink even more. After dinner, most everyone retreated to their rooms, ending yet another day of uncertainty.

Len and I took a walk to the riverbank. I wanted to share what had happened, but he'd had his own adventures.

"I met my wife today," he said.

"Um, what?" I must have misheard him. He told me just the previous night he'd been married for forty years.

"It's Gretchen. She's in the group."

He had to be joking, but his tone was both serious and excited. I had no idea where he was going with that information. I was trying to remember which one of the ladies she was.

"Yeah, she did a past life regression with me. Turns out, she's my wife from one of my previous lives. We were married about three thousand years ago. Unfortunately, I died in battle. We had two daughters, and—"

"Len, come on," I blurted out. "Forget about something that happened in the past. Or didn't. We have a much more pressing matter at hand."

He didn't let up. I listened with borrowed patience—I was so much more interested in what was happening in this life. I zoned out, picturing myself returning happily to the monotony of driving thirty minutes on the highway to work each morning before the crack of dawn. I could picture the smooth, black, newly laid asphalt that made driving my pickup truck a real pleasure. I realised Len had stopped talking.

"I have a plan to get us out of here," I said. "Are you on board?"

Len's eyes narrowed, and he tilted his head forward in submission. "Go on. I'm listening." Finally, the roaring lion had been tamed.

"The entire plan may depend on Marilyn buying into it."

"Marilyn? Who cares what she says? She's really just another participant like us. God bless her. I wouldn't want to be in her position. There are some real crazies in this group. I wouldn't want the job of trying to wrangle all of them. At dinner today, some lady yelled at me."

By then, I knew enough about Len to understand he wasn't afraid to speak his mind. He'd ruffled quite a few feathers with his prayer performance earlier. I wasn't all that surprised to hear someone else had taken offense to one of his actions.

"The bitch got in my face and screeched that I had failed to wash my plate properly. What the hell?"

"What's there to washing a plate?" I asked, dumbfounded. I couldn't believe anyone would make a fuss over something like that, given our situation.

"Exactly! I'm sure she was just venting her frustration, but I don't accept being treated like that. I didn't back down from her. Nope, I told her off."

Marilyn had her own growing clique and mini support system. I was afraid the dishwashing exchange was already being relayed to her, likely with embellishments. It wasn't going to help Len and me sell her on my idea.

"Len, just forget it for now," I begged. "Please, focus. Let's talk about the plan. Then we can present it to the group. Here's what I—"

"Let's do an affirmation about the plan."

"You don't even know what it is yet."

Len went ahead with his affirmation. "I surrender to the Infinite Wisdom, and it will guide us. Know it, we will make it out of here." He then said, "Niranjan, you and I are a unit. I've already visualised the two of us getting everyone out safely. You know what, I'll also submit my application to the universe that we'll leave here two days from now. If the rest decide to stay back and want to continue to listen to Marilyn and her useless ideas, so be it. You and I are gone. Off this mountain—off to our next adventure."

I had no desire to remind Len we had yet to make our current one a success. I was the pragmatic one; Len was unbound and carefree. There I was, trying to save our lives, and he was more interested in his three-thousand-year-old wife and the brewing drama within our group.

Who could I turn to for help? Guru Ananda was lost in his own blissful world. As far as he was concerned, the Himalayas were simply a waiting room that eventually led to transcendental heaven. He had no worldly ties and would happily spend the rest of his life in that spot. I was frustrated.

I needed a serious partner for my plans. I didn't want to have to do it all on my own.

"Never mind," I told Len.

Chapter 20

Thwhip, thwhip, thwhip.

I woke with a start. A helicopter buzzed overhead, its powerful blades spinning through the thin mountain air. It was past 7:00 a.m. I'd missed the morning yoga and meditation, but I didn't care. I heard one more helicopter, and then another, their noise ricocheting off the rock face and surrounding mountains. Every few seconds, another one came, only to fade away again.

I hurried outside, joining the throng that had emerged from the meditation hall. Everyone was waving frantically to the sky. I imagined the tens of thousands of survivors stranded all over the mountains doing the same thing. I didn't know how many people those helicopters could hold, but even if it were thirty or forty, the rescue effort would move in slow motion.

Marilyn was back on the phone. Her free hand was moving in all directions as she screamed, "Where is our chopper? We were promised rescue days ago! Don't they know we're all foreigners here? Why aren't we on the top of their list? I need answers now."

Guru Ananda's gaze was settled calmly on the high, churning waters of the river. He paid little attention to the action above us. BJ had his eyes closed and was moving through his morning calisthenics routine. Every once in a while, he would pause and clutch his back. I was the only one who seemed to notice.

Len spotted me and rushed to my side. "Is this your plan? Wow, what a spectacle!"

The helicopters were flying so low we could almost see the pilots.

"No, Len, it's not. They can't land here. We're waiting in place for nothing."

Len looked disappointed. "What a story it would be, though, to tell my congregants back in Dallas—how I flew off the mountains after a life-threatening flood."

"Oh, don't worry, you'll get your helicopter ride, but we have to make it to them first. Wait here while I speak to Guru Ananda."

I had rehearsed in my head what I was going to say. Short, precise, and to the point. No loose ends. I knew Marilyn would jump in and try to shoot down the idea down before it reached the guru's ears, but I had to try.

"Namaste, Guruji. Jim and I went up—" I began.

"Why did you return so late yesterday?" Marilyn admonished me.

I ignored her and looked straight into my teacher's eyes. "We are lucky to be alive. A landslide pushed the river away from us." I was breathing hard. The prepared speech disappeared from my mind. "We met a few locals—"

"Who were they? Where did you meet them?" Marilyn was beginning to grill me. Things were not going as planned.

Guru Ananda turned to Marilyn and raised his hand. She stopped talking, but I could tell she was gritting her teeth. BJ gave me a curious stare. I presumed he was in support of

Marilyn. I sensed he preferred the easy way out, where help simply lowered itself out of the sky to the ashram's doorstep. I couldn't imagine him toiling through the muddy forest and climbing over downed trees in his white dhoti.

I truly hoped that once I told Guru Ananda about Ram, he would understand that staying there wasn't the best option.

"The villagers didn't need our medicines," I continued, "but they desperately needed food. I gave them some of ours."

"You did what?" Marilyn could not contain herself. She nudged BJ to go check how much was left. "If getting out of here wasn't hard enough, now you've added another problem. My God. I can't take this anymore." She scrunched up her face and started rubbing her temples.

"Let me explain, please! I met Ram—"

"Who's Ram?" she hissed. She was turning outright venomous.

"Ram is a man—"

"I know it's a man's name." Marilyn would neither listen nor let me talk. I was seething inside.

"He can get us out of here." I attempted again, ready to plough through Marilyn with my words if she interrupted me once more.

"How do you know?" she challenged, her eyes narrowing like the pupils of a pit viper.

"Gut instinct."

"Jesus Christ. I need more than a gut feeling if we are all going to risk our lives with your scheme. Let me tell you what my gut says. To stay here and get rescued properly by people in uniforms. Not by some Ram from the woods. We can't have everyone making decisions for themselves. I make the decisions."

I was getting nowhere. "All right, I apologise. I will fold and go with what the group decides." I had no intention of folding, but I was certainly done with Marilyn.

BJ returned and reeled off what was left of the rations. Marilyn barked at him to go back and ask the cooks how long it would last.

Guru Ananda didn't say a word. He was lost in a world detached from our lowly human concerns. His attention was on a greater prize. The retreat participants were operating from the lowest chakra, the Mooladhara, which governed food and survival. But he was at the door of the highest chakra, the Sahasrara—the thousand-petaled lotus. I followed his gaze to the giant SOS sign Len and I had laid out on the sandy riverbank. Surprisingly, it was still intact. I wondered if any of the pilots had seen it as I turned to go to the dining hall.

Breakfast was delayed due to all the excitement of the morning. By the time I arrived, everyone was gathered in groups of three or four, chattering away as if the mere appearance of so many helicopters meant we were already rescued. I desperately wanted to talk to Len, but he was nowhere to be seen. Perhaps he was with Gretchen—they had a lot of catching up to do. I was rummaging through my rucksack when I heard the voice of the only person I didn't feel like talking to.

"What are you doing now?" Marilyn snapped accusingly. I was officially in her crosshairs.

"I'm just looking for my chocolate."

"You have chocolate with you?" Her voice sweetened and shot up an octave. She was suddenly smiling. I'd never seen her smile; she was practically unrecognisable. I seized the opportunity, hoping to bribe her, and hastily turned my rucksack upside down. Out came two bars of precious organic dark chocolate. Perhaps that was the way back into her good graces. I held up both and let her pick. She chose the one with 50 percent cacao and left the bitter one for me.

"Mmm, this is so good," she drawled. "It's been such a long time." She lovingly munched on the bar with her eyes closed.

I sensed an opening. Perhaps she would be nicer while she was floating somewhere closer to the Sahasrara chakra. "So, what do you do in the States?" I asked.

Her scowl returned as soon as she swallowed her last bite.

"That was a different life. A different time. I can't talk about it."

"Sorry, I just—"

"That's okay. Thanks for the chocolate." And she left.

I heard Len's voice outside. He was standing on a large, flat stone, speaking to a small assemblage. Len had a magnetic personality that was slowly drawing more people in. Unfortunately, he had also attracted Marilyn's attention. She sent BJ to investigate his activity and report back. Perhaps she worried about Len staging a coup. More than likely, though, it was another long-winded prayer or affirmation. It was obvious he loved to hold court. The bigger the audience, the better. I stood at the back to listen in. Len was thrilled to see I was in attendance, and he asked me to come forward, pulling me up next to him like a prop.

"Niranjan is going to lead us out of here! Mark my words, in two days, we'll leave this place, come hell or high water. Our application to the universe has been submitted. Consider it as good as done!" I tried to shrink myself, but I was a few

169

inches taller than Len and had no place to hide. I met BJ's eyes in the crowd. He was glaring at me.

Suddenly, queries from the crowd were lobbed at us thick and fast like we were elected officials responding to press reporters. The masses were desperate for information. Len fielded all the questions with utmost confidence, and just like a politician, he answered without actually answering. He kept mentioning the plan but divulged no real details since there were none yet. The entire scheme, as Marilyn had called it, depended entirely on Ram's willingness to help us find an appropriate place to attract a helicopter. I'd have to hike up the mountain again to find him.

I'd heard enough. I needed to clear my head, so I snuck away while Len continued on about his life in Dallas, his ministry, and his college days. I wondered if anyone was actually buying what he was selling.

I got myself a cup of watered-down tea, which tasted like a combination of wild roots and grass, and sat in a quiet spot outside. Suddenly, a familiar face came into view. Ram. You could have convinced me I was seeing the face of God. The key to our escape had just appeared for everyone to see. He headed straight for Guru Ananda, whose ochre robes unmistakably signified he was the person of most importance. I thrust my cup into the unsuspecting hands of an approaching Len and asked him to wash it for me. Before he could respond, I was halfway to Ram, who had returned to properly thank Guru Ananda for the rice and lentils. He paid his respects in the traditional Indian way, by kneeling with his forehead to the ground while touching the guru's feet.

Marilyn was nowhere to be seen, so I was able to speak freely and give Guru Ananda a glowing testimonial of Ram's trekking and navigation abilities. I also relayed how he had saved me from tumbling down the side of the mountain. Guru Ananda simply smiled and contributed an occasional 'hmm'.

"Sir," Ram said, looking at me. "We have word from other locals that members of the Indo-Tibetan Border Police are in the area with helicopters." The ITBP were normally used to patrol the border between India and China but were also designated as first responders during natural disasters.

"They have set up a field station to transfer flood refugees," he claimed.

"How far away is it?" I asked, hope rising through the knot that had been in my stomach for days.

"It's several kilometres downriver, just past the dam. Many people from my village have already started to build a trail in that direction."

"How long do you think it would take us to get there?" I asked.

"I'm not sure. Probably six hours of walking. The terrain is difficult."

I didn't need to hear any more. I gave him three hundred rupees from my wallet and hired him as our guide. No need to consult Marilyn. Our group was about to fracture in two—those who were with me and those who were with Marilyn. Up to that point, Len and Ram were the only ones on my side, but that was plenty. I asked Ram to return the next morning to take Len and me on an exploratory trek to determine if it was something everyone in the group could manage.

After Ram left, BJ slid up to me. "You are a troublemaker," he declared. I stood expressionless, waiting for more. "If you want to go, just leave, but don't bring others into your plans. You can run away quietly in the middle of the night for all I care, but we have a plan. To stay put and follow Marilyn's directions."

"What kind of plan is that?" I retorted. "What are we supposed to do? Hope the military eventually air-drops some food? Wait a few months until the roads are all cleared and repaired? Then maybe someone will bring us materials to rebuild the bridge so we can drive back down the mountain? Or do we wait until the monsoon season is over and hope someone can come get us in a boat? No, no, I'm not doing that. You can, if you want, but I'm going to find a helicopter."

I couldn't tell if BJ was considering my response or not. I hoped he would understand my point of view. He grabbed his back again.

"Is your back okay?" I asked.

My question threw him off guard. "It's fine," he stammered. He leaned in a little closer, pointing at my chest. "I'll be watching you."

Chapter 21

The next morning, Tapovana was alive with chatter about the mystery guide who would lead us to safety. I couldn't believe it. The previous night, I had told Len—in confidence—about Ram's willingness to try and get us to the ITBP field station. Len must have entrusted his ancient wife with the information, and she, in turn, told everyone else. Even Marilyn knew. Her cold-blooded stares from the breakfast line said it all.

"Ahhh, the plan to escape," Jacques said approvingly as he sat down next to me in the dining hall. "Well done. I have my own plan."

"Really? What is it?" I probed. Perhaps he had some good ideas. I was hoping to recruit him to my team. He was strong. I knew he would be more than capable of holding his own on our trek that morning.

"I want to swim across the river. I made some calculations—the number of strokes times the distance. I think I can do it. I used to be a lifeguard."

I was shocked. The thrashing current was deadly. It would be impossible for even the most capable swimmer. "Jacques, you have no life jacket. It's far too dangerous. Besides, what would you do once you made it to the other side?" I made my best effort not to sound like a smart ass. The opposite bank was as much a dead end as the retreat centre.

"I'd call for help, yes?" Jacques replied matter-of-factly. "Marilyn, she is not helping us. We must do something more than sit here."

"Yes, I agree that we need to act on our own. Why don't you join Len and me on our hike this morning?" Jacques would be good company to have along. Plus, he possessed the most important qualification: he was highly motivated to leave.

Jacques was instantly on board, and I requested that he not invite anyone else. I had no idea what to expect on our journey, but I knew it would involve hours of walking. If the terrain was anything like my last tromp up the mountain, the other group members would be much better off saving their strength. There was no reason to expend unnecessary energy—especially considering our scant meal portions.

"Excuse me," interrupted a woman's voice.

Jacques and I lifted our chins to find a tall, willowy American woman with red hair and freckles standing over us. She was wearing a walking cast.

"Sarah, good morning!" Jacques exclaimed warmly. "Have you met Niranjan?"

"Not officially, no."

I stood up and shook her hand. "Hi, it's nice to meet you. What happened to your leg?"

She winced as if reliving the memory. "I broke my foot a few days before the trip. I almost decided not to come. I probably would have been better off at home, huh?"

"Yeah, this has been pretty crazy," I agreed.

Jacques jumped to his feet. "Niranjan is taking us to the helicopters."

"So the rumours are true." Sarah grinned.

"Well, kind of," I said. "We need to figure out if the route to the field station would be navigable by everyone."

Sarah instinctively glanced at her foot. "Yeah, that's what I wanted to talk to you about. I would really like to leave, and normally I wouldn't mind hiking out, but I don't think I'll make it very far in this boot."

"I agree. Tell you what, if I'm able to make contact with the military camp today, I'll let them know we have someone here who's injured. Maybe they can figure out a solution for you."

"Okay, thank you," Sarah said. "Please let me know what they say."

"I will. I promise."

Jacques excused himself and dashed over to his friends who were exiting the dining hall. I couldn't hear what he was saying, but his sweeping gestures revealed that he was unable to contain his excitement. I knew exactly what was happening. Sure enough, about fifteen minutes later, Jacques and a handful of his friends returned to the dining hall with backpacks and various forms of walking sticks. I panicked and ran to find Len, who was inspecting our SOS sign down by the river.

"I think I messed up," I blurted.

"What happened?" Len asked.

"I invited Jacques to accompany us today."

"That's a great idea! What's the problem?"

"He's invited five more people! I don't think they should come. This isn't a picnic party or some leisurely day hike. It could be really difficult. The fewer people, the better. Don't you think? Will you please go talk to Jacques and sort this all out?"

"Oh, no, no, no," Len said firmly. "I'm not doing it. You're the brains behind this whole operation. You've gotta be bold and speak up. Tell the ones who want to join us, in no uncertain terms, that it's a no-go." Len pressed his lips together in a tight grin and raised his eyebrows expectantly. He wouldn't let me back away from my fear of telling people no.

I grudgingly agreed to address the pack of willing trailblazers, but I made Len come with me in case I required backup. I stood in front of them, acknowledging each of their expectant faces. "Hey, guys. It's likely to be about twelve hours of walking today, round trip. I feel like having too many people along will just slow us down. I only want to take Jacques and Len."

They grumbled a little but nodded. They understood. I was relieved they didn't plead their case. It was hard enough to say no once. I couldn't imagine having to do it repeatedly. Len flashed me a thumbs up and a smile.

The minutes rolled by, but Ram hadn't shown up yet. Meanwhile, a handful of group members who had switched to Team Niranjan were gathering around to wish us a safe journey. Marilyn looked on with her ever-present frown. I grabbed Len's arm and pulled him into our room.

"What's going on?" he asked.

"Sorry, I had to get away from Marilyn. I can't stand the way she's always staring at us like she's about to strike."

"Amen," he agreed.

"What do you think we should take with us today? I'm going to bring my water bottle. It has a filter in case we need to drink stream water."

"I'm bringing all my essentials in case we can't return," Len said. "You know, my passport, my money, my phone—just the things that will help me get back home."

He had a zippered leather fanny pack that never left his waist. Carefully, he tucked his three most important possessions inside. My hospital scrub pockets didn't have zippers. I wanted to take my passport and money but envisioned everything falling out somewhere along the trail, unbeknownst to me.

"Could you carry my things in your pack?" I asked hopefully.

"Aw, come on. What do I look like, your wife?" He sounded serious. Then he cracked a smile. "Just kidding. Anything for you, my brother. We're in this together."

By then, it was close to 11:00 a.m. There was still no sign of Ram. He'd been sincere when he promised to return, and I knew he was trustworthy. I also knew he didn't have a watch, so I was hoping he'd just lost track of time and was on his way. Darkness didn't faze him, so he would have no qualms about leaving that afternoon. At least, I would be able to put another meal in my stomach before heading into the unknown.

Marilyn found me at lunch and brusquely pulled me aside. She had caught her prey. It was humiliating to be singled out and led from the dining hall like a little kid in trouble. Len jumped to his feet and came to my rescue before she could pull me through the door. "Hang on, sister!" he yelled to Marilyn, holding his hand up and willing her to stop. He wasn't afraid of a head-on confrontation in the middle of the lunchroom. "If this is about the trek today—to save us—you've gotta let us go."

Marilyn spun around, her face contorted, eyes wild. She had finally met her match in Len. "I don't care what the two of you do! If you want to go get lost in the mountains, be my guest! But everyone else is staying here with me." She was trembling with rage.

"Why are you making this so hard?" Len shot back. "You should be thanking Niranjan for having the intelligence and bravery to come up with a way out of here before we all rot! Instead, you're treating him like a criminal! I won't have it! Shame on you!"

The room had fallen completely silent, and everyone sat slack-jawed. I spied Jacques out of the corner of my eye. He was shaking his head slowly and mouthing the word no. He had changed his mind about going. He was more scared of Marilyn than the possibility of getting lost in the wild Himalayas.

Len and Marilyn were facing off, eye to eye. The lion versus the snake. I wondered who would back down first. Marilyn eventually turned and retreated.

It was half-past two before Ram finally arrived. He apologised profusely. He had been working at a frenetic pace with other villagers to get the new trail made. Not only to help us, but to help themselves. Their livelihoods depended on access to the valley.

"Ram, I'm a little worried about leaving so late. We won't be able to make it back before dark."

"It's okay, sir. It's better that we didn't leave earlier. We would have become stranded in a very dangerous place. The villagers are working now to make it passable. It should be okay by the time we get there. You will see for yourself. It is very bad."

Len and I set off with Ram, our supporters standing at the edge of the ashram grounds to see us off. They waved as we faded into the dense forest. Ram started jogging barefoot over the uneven, rocky terrain as if he were in running shoes on a city sidewalk.

"Can you slow down a little?" I gasped, my ankles wobbling on the stones. I could hear Len behind me, breathing hard. "We aren't used to this thin air and rough ground."

"Okay, sir, but please try to hurry. We have a very long way to go," replied Ram.

After a few minutes under the thick canopy of trees, we emerged out into the open. Making a sharp turn back towards the river, I could see what little remained of the trail the villagers had frequented before the storm. Most of it was under a landslide, buried deep in a slanted hill of mud. One slip would have landed us in the agitated waters below.

Soon we were faced with an eight-foot dirt wall. Ram scrambled up effortlessly—like a mountain goat. I was flabbergasted. I was convinced locals had specialised adaptations on the soles of their feet. My hiking boots were practically useless in comparison. I couldn't get up the wall, no matter how hard I tried. It was too steep and slippery.

Seeing my difficulty, Ram clambered back down and broke a fallen tree branch into sticks about a foot long. Using a stone, he hammered them into the wall, making a rudimentary ladder for us. He cautioned us about putting too much weight on any one peg. His invention worked. Len and I were able to climb up the wall onto a rocky ledge that wound around the edge of the mountain. There was nothing there to break our fall if we slipped—just the unforgiving vertical face of the mountain below.

Every step I took on that ledge, I double and triple checked my footing. Len was still right behind me. Ram warned us not to hold on to each other as we worked our way across the narrow span that connected back around to a section of trail that was still intact. If one of us went down, the other would follow. I was impressed with Len's ability to keep up, and his nerves were surprisingly resilient. It was evident he had the energy of a thirty-year-old and the enthusiasm of a teenager.

We continued up and down several ridges. Below us, in the distance, I could see villagers scattered in different sections of the mountain attempting to salvage parts of the trail. They were working in perilous conditions. Squatting down low with their knees sticking up, they worked with their hands to dig the path and clear the way. Their progress was moving at a crawl, but what other option did they have?

Len and I had been slipping and sliding randomly along the way. My boots were getting heavier as they became saturated with water and caked with mud. It occurred to me that Ram hadn't slipped—not even once. I decided to follow him precisely by stepping in his tracks. It helped keep me steady. I envied Ram's bare feet and dared not take my eyes off them. I wondered if I should take off my shoes.

"How are you doing, Len?" I called behind me. "Having fun?"

"Just another day in paradise," he replied between two deep gasps. "I can't believe everything we're witnessing."

"Look what's ahead." I pointed to a steep incline that headed straight up the mountainside.

Ram paused, surveying the obstacles that lay ahead. Although he wasn't very old, his weather-beaten skin had fine facial lines that were accentuated by his frequent squinting as he considered our options. He wasn't just assessing the walkability of the trail but also weighing the chances of us setting off a landslide. Many of his friends and relatives were working below us.

"Can we get up there?" I asked Ram.

He answered in English for Len's sake. "Sirs, very difficult. I climb, no problem. You stay here?" he asked, half pleading.

"Hold on," Len said. "I'm no quitter. We're going with you." He was adamant.

"We will follow your lead and guidance," I said. "But please, we must come. We have to establish contact with the military camp." We were already covered in mud by that point. Our haggard appearance would speak for us once we arrived. Hopefully, someone in charge would take pity on us and develop a quick, efficient, simple rescue strategy that we hadn't thought of. Len and I were having a difficult time with the trek. I wasn't sure how the rest of the group would be able to manage.

"How much farther?" I asked Ram.

"Not too far, sir. But there is no more trail from here on out." He pointed to several high ridges we still had to cross. "We have to push through the forest. I don't know how long it will take."

Ram reluctantly agreed to let us follow him on the steep incline. I couldn't tell how far up it reached. It was shrouded in clouds.

I looked down behind me to check on Len and saw the enormity of our situation. "Hey, Len, how far do you think it is to the bottom? Five hundred feet?"

"Nah," he replied, judging it carefully. "Probably more like eight hundred. This is the real juice of life, isn't it? Man, oh, man." Unlike me, he was dialled in for the adventure. I, personally, was not excited by any of it. I just wanted to get home. I don't think I would have had the energy or the courage to do it without Len by my side.

My quads burned as we slogged up. And up. And up.

"Stop!" Ram shouted. "Watch out here! The ground is gone! You see, this is the bad part!"

We began to wind around a narrow rock outcrop, and not too far ahead, I could see what Ram was warning us about. Part of the outcrop had fallen away. There was a gap about fifteen feet across between us and the other side.

Len let out a low whistle. "Would you look at that," he said softly.

I didn't know if he was talking about the actual gap or the two rotting logs someone had laid across in an effort to make a bridge. The logs weren't secured by anything, just wedged between rocks on either end. Crossing would require not only courage but balance as well. I had a horrible sense of balance, and I knew my clumpy boots would make it worse. I looked at Ram, who was built for living in those parts. He would have no trouble. He was short and had a low centre of gravity. Hell, his toes were practically claws. Surprising no one, Ram made it across in the blink of an eye.

He waited on the other end, facing us and beckoning with one hand while pointing with the other where he thought we should place our first step. The key was forward progress without thinking or hesitation. Len stood silently behind me as a serious mood descended on both of us. There was no turning back. In that moment, I felt I'd rather plunge to my death on the side of the sacred mountain than endure another day of Marilyn. *Now or never.* I strode across, pretending to be calm, and uneventfully arrived at the other side. Len followed immediately. We looked at each other in amazement and relief but didn't have time or energy to celebrate.

From that point, we picked our way slowly down the mountain, and as we descended out of the clouds, the river was visible once again. We would follow it all the way to the dam, staying several hundred feet above it. We manoeuvred our way over cliff edges and narrow spots. There was no room for complacency. Many considerations were taken before each step, and I found the mental aspect of our trek to be an unexpected drain on our stamina.

I gulped the rest of my water as we came upon a relatively flat, grassy area, and I rested my aching body on a boulder. Len was a short distance away, relaxing on the rock of his choice. I closed my eyes and began to daydream about my bed at home. When I opened my eyes, Ram was gone. Len was lost in his own thoughts, sitting in a meditative pose. His eyes were closed, his sunglasses perched on his head just where his receding hairline started. I shook him out of his trance.

"Where's Ram?" I asked, my voice suddenly tight. It was unlike him to simply disappear. Possibilities raced through my mind. Maybe he fell down the mountain while I had my eyes closed. Maybe he decided not to help us and left us in the middle of nowhere. Maybe he was silently snatched by a tiger. "Len!" I squawked. "What are were going to do?"

At least, we had a view of the river below us. I knew if we continued to follow it, we would eventually encounter human habitation. The dam also occasionally came into view. On the opposite bank, I could see the highway that connected to Rishikesh, a few tea stalls, and lodging houses sprinkled along the roadside.

"I'm sure he'll be back," Len said, closing his eyes again.

After about forty minutes, Ram came jogging around the corner with a couple of water bottles. He had found civilisation. As soon as he saw us, he started yelling, "Sirs, danger! You must move!" Len and I jumped to our feet. Ram pointed up the mountain behind us, then down to the rocks on the ground, including the boulders we had been resting on. "Landslides. They can come back any time. Not a good place to stop. The dam is a twenty-minute walk from here. We are very close now. Let's go."

Refreshed by the rest and fluids, we pressed on. It wasn't long before we took a turn that brought the dam into full view. It had survived the storm. It was fully intact, with a paved road over its entire expanse. We would have no trouble making it to the other side of the river.

Halfway across, I gave Len my camera so I could pose for a photo. I could see that the small zoom lens was sticking out to its fullest length, but Len wasn't taking a picture. He was using it to survey the damage to the highway behind me.

"Niranjan, the road we took to come up here no longer exists," he said.

"What? Maybe you just can't see it from here," I suggested.

"No. You don't understand. Here, look for yourself." He thrust the camera into my face and held it up to eye level. His hands were shaking from exhaustion and caloric deficit.

"I can't see, Len. Stop shaking so much."

I grabbed the camera from him for a better look. Ram held a puzzled expression on his face. We looked like two tourists squabbling over a photograph while there were more important items on the agenda. I finally saw it. Entire sections of the main road were missing, replaced by river water whipping what was left of the road.

We promptly finished crossing, joyful to finally be standing on the opposite bank. It took me a minute to realise the military field station was nowhere in sight.

Chapter 22

Ram made inquiries at the tea stall where he had bought the water and was able to confirm the presence of a military camp nearby. We were urged to make our way there quickly, before dark. I was famished, but eating would have to wait. I tried to calculate how many calories I must have burned while going over the mountains, but my brain refused to cooperate. My leg muscles were burning, my knees trembling, but I shuffled ahead with urgency while pleading with Len not to give up. He was fading fast. I was concerned he wouldn't hold up on the return trip. I prayed he could be rejuvenated by a decent meal. Perhaps Ram could find a local to feed us some home cooking. I let the thought linger in my mind, where it conjured up a unique aroma and pleasant aftertaste. I was hallucinating.

"Hang in there, Len," I begged. "We'll be there soon."

It was the miracle of modern engineering that had kept the dam standing. Everything else was a picture of complete destruction. We made our way carefully down the broken road, picking our way closer to the camp, avoiding the deep, watery pits and jutting cracks.

"I see it!" Ram shouted, running ahead. Len and I followed, painstakingly pushing through a thicket of shrubs and toppled trees only to stumble out into a huge clearing. A single small helicopter with drooping blades sat in front of a damaged old building. Where were the other helicopters? Where were all the troops? On the far side of the field, thousands of people waited. They were standing, sitting, and squatting. A few were stretched out on blankets. Women huddled together around cooking fires and makeshift stoves.

A large, muscular Indian man in army fatigues marked ITBP stood near the four-seater helicopter, directing newly arriving refugees to the far end of the clearing. He was obviously in charge. He had a thick, well-groomed handlebar moustache and dark eyes. I imagined he would appear menacing to any invaders trying to cross the border.

As we approached the commander, I asked Len to do the talking. Normally, that wasn't something he would need encouragement with, but he was spent. I told him it was important—his American status and silver hair would put him at the top of the list for evacuation. I hoped the way his hair was styled would set the tone for our plea. It was sticking straight up, held in place by drying globs of mud. Even if the commander didn't speak English, few words would be needed to get Len's desperate message out.

"We need help," Len croaked, wincing and rubbing his forehead. The bit of added drama was a nice touch.

The commander replied easily in English. "Please, tell me."

"There are about forty of us at a meditation retreat centre. On the other bank, up the river a ways," continued Len, flopping his arm in the air half-heartedly.

The commander eyed our dirty clothes and dishevelled condition. "We have been running sorties every thirty minutes to temporary refugee shelters, where people are given food and tents. Since you're a foreigner, you have priority." Len's face was his passport. I whipped out mine to prove I also met the requirements for expedited transfer.

A soldier appeared, handing each of us a food packet and a sealed sachet of mango juice. I was so grateful I felt like crying. I didn't want to be rude and stuff my face while trying to speak to the commander, but at that point, I was feeling light-headed. I drained the mango juice and wolfed down the oily bread and potatoes.

"This is the last flight of the day," the commander said, pointing to the little helicopter. "It's leaving in ten minutes. I can put you both on it if you want. You don't have any bags, do you?"

"No, we don't," I answered.

"Good. We are not allowing luggage on the flights. Just small personal items like wallets, purses, phones…"

I turned to Len to see what he wanted to do. I was tempted to accept the ride, but I knew it was wrong. Even though they didn't seem to realise it, our group at the ashram needed us to return with that information.

"No, we won't be going," Len replied. "We can't leave our friends like that. Their survival depends on us. We will bring them here."

"I've seen bigger helicopters than this one. Will there be larger rescue flights?" I asked hopefully.

"Yes, but not until the day after tomorrow. Today we had limited flights to work out our logistics. There are countless individuals stranded in all parts of these mountains." Pointing to the mass of humanity lining the field, he said, "These are just a few of the lucky ones. Too many others are waiting in place. This is going to be a massive rescue operation. We will likely have to start with food drops for those we can't get to soon enough."

I remembered Sarah. "We have a woman in our group who is injured. She has a broken foot and will not be able to walk back here with us. Do you know how we can get her out? I don't think a regular helicopter will be able to land where we are. The only flat area near us is a tiny bit of the riverbank. It's sandy and still partially flooded."

"Anyone injured has top priority. Do you have a phone?"

"Yes, there's a satellite phone at the retreat centre."

"Good," he said. "Call and make arrangements. We will send our smallest helicopter to complete a flyover and see what the options are. If it's safe to land, we will pick her up and bring her here."

"Do you think there might be any way the smallest one could come get all of us, a couple at a time, and drop us off here for transfer? It's a strenuous six-hour walk from where we are staying."

"We aren't set up to do that now. The smaller choppers are for the injured and short sorties to the next camp. I don't know when they would be available to come get you. It would probably be a few weeks at least."

We had no choice but to return and try to convince Marilyn that the best option was a trek to the field station. If we couldn't talk her into it, I was determined to bring whoever was willing to disobey her. I thanked the commander and promised we would be back in two days with more people. Before we left, the soldier handing out the food gave us each an extra pack to take with us—may he live forever.

Our weary bodies cast long shadows on the remnants of the road as we carefully retraced our steps to the dam. The silver paint on the deserted guard tower shimmered in the setting sun. We sat down in the middle of the pavement that spanned the dam and took a few precious minutes to eat. I unwrapped the wrinkled silver paper and found a bun stuffed with spiced potatoes. I was delighted to secure another dose of carbs. I would need the boost on the way back. I peeked at Len's package and was relieved to see he would be able to carb load as well. We ate quickly, anxious to conquer all the hazards of the return trip. Even Ram seemed a little uneasy. It was unfamiliar territory for him. There had been a few forks in the trail along the way he was uncertain about. In the daylight, he was able to make educated guesses based on his surroundings. At night, everything would look different. I was terrified we would get lost and have to spend the night in the woods.

I freed my headlamp from one of my scrub pockets and secured it in the region of my third eye. If only the light could also shine inward and allow me to see through the darkness that lay within. Len held a pencil-thin flashlight that projected an intense, narrow ray. Ram was ecstatic upon discovering our lighting options. He suggested I lead the way since my beam was wider. I declined but let him wear my headlamp. I would follow his footsteps closely, and Len would bring up the rear.

The way back was unrecognisable. Shadows danced around us as our fearless lights fought against the entirety of the darkness. I could barely see a couple of feet in front of me, and the headlamp lit up about four feet in front of Ram. I reminded him to proceed slowly so we wouldn't lose track of him and prayed the flashlights wouldn't fail.

Up and down, over and around I stumbled, walking numbly, considering each step a small victory. Len slipped and fell a few times. I could tell when he went down because the beam of his flashlight would suddenly shoot up to the sky. Ram equipped him with a sturdy tree branch to use as a walking stick. I elected to keep both my hands free in case I needed to grab on to something. Len and I struggled to keep up with the endless march, but Ram showed no signs of tiring. He let us rest for a few minutes once he determined it was safe to do so. Unlike me, he knew better than to take a pit stop on a recent landslide. Len's watch read 8:30 p.m. If we maintained our pace, we could make it back to the ashram around midnight.

Len was too tired to talk. An extrovert by nature, the silence was unusual for him—if not for the beam of light shining from his hand, I wouldn't have been able to tell he was behind me.

I tried to listen for his footsteps, but my ears were humming from the calls of the crickets. I tried to match the pace of my steps to the rise and fall of their sound, but right when I would catch the pattern, it would change. I chose to keep my mind trained on the noise of the harmless insects. It was much more pleasant than thinking about what else might be moving around in the wild night.

To complicate matters, it began to rain. It made the ground extremely slick. Ram slowed his pace. He sensed the additional threat it could present in the dark. Len hollered as he fell again. That time, the beam from his flashlight completely disappeared. Ram and I froze.

"Len?" I called out. There was no answer. Ram swung into action, squeezing by me with the headlamp to illuminate the spot where Len had been. He was gone. Terror raced through me as Ram peered over the edge of the drop-off. There was Len, about three feet down, splayed flat and tangled in a young tree that was sticking sideways out of the mountain. He was still with us—and extraordinarily lucky the tree decided to catch him.

With the precision of a surgeon, Ram took his time helping Len extricate himself from the branches. I did a quick check for sprained body parts and broken bones. He was scratched up and badly shaken, but I gave him the all-clear to keep walking. His flashlight had not survived. With one light left in front, I switched places with Len to bring up the rear. Ram held Len's hand the rest of the way. I was happy to discover the back of Len's shirt had a tiny strip of reflective material. In the daytime, it looked like part of the pattern, but in the dark, it was my guide. The clouds parted now and then, allowing the dull glow of the moon to reflect off his back and give me a visual on Ram and Len. One wrong turn, and we could easily be separated.

Once we came to the eight-foot dirt wall, I knew the ashram was close. Ram descended first and helped us to the bottom. He still looked to be in good shape, but I was delirious with exhaustion.

Ram dropped us off at the dining hall. We insisted he spend the night so he wouldn't have to walk home, but he would have none of that. I urged him to keep my headlamp at least, and for that, he was grateful. I asked if he could return the next day and join us in presenting our new information to Marilyn and Guru Ananda. Everyone was sleeping by the time

Len and I collapsed onto our thin mattresses. I wondered if anyone had worried about us while we were gone. Len whispered something I couldn't decipher, and we instantly fell asleep.

Chapter 23

Unbearable itching woke me before sunrise. I started to sit up, but that made my head throb. Every cell in my body was hurting. I had to brace myself from head to toe to make the slightest adjustments in bed. I couldn't reach down to investigate what was causing the itch, so I ran my right foot over my left leg, and I found a surprise. Several of them, actually. Soft, fleshy bumps covered my ankles. A cold shiver ran up my spine, my grogginess gone in an instant. What the heck was on my legs? It was completely dark in the room. Len was sound asleep, his flashlight somewhere in the wilderness. My headlamp had left the previous night with Ram's forehead.

The other leg also had a few bumps around the ankle. *My God, it's some type of giant jungle tick!* I would have to wait until the morning to find out what they looked like. I told myself I needed more rest, but I was wide awake. Between revolving emotions of fear, disgust, and confusion, I employed various techniques to calm myself and fall asleep again. I began by counting backwards from ninety-nine to one and ended by trying to remember the names of all our sheep back home. Nothing worked. I was pleading for mercy from aloof gods, making innumerable promises of repentance. I was being eaten alive as I lay there helpless, and there was nothing I could do about it.

My mind took off running as I imagined everyone hiking out on foot, leaving me behind, incapacitated by my jungle ticks. My emaciated frame would have to be carted away by army medics in the little droopy helicopter. Specialists would be called in only to tell me the creatures couldn't be removed. They would simply have to get their fill and fall off on their own.

I squeezed the chub on my belly to see how much more of myself I could afford to feed them. I turned my head slowly to see Len sleeping peacefully. He was wearing long johns and thick woollen socks. I couldn't see his feet; perhaps he was spared the same nightmare. I was thankful for that. At least, sweet Len would survive to tell my story. I wished we had accepted the ITBP commander's offer to leave on the last flight out.

Daybreak couldn't come fast enough. As soon as the first speck of light filtered in through the far window, I hefted one of my legs up in the air, trying not to groan. Finally, I could confront the little aliens. Flat discs, bulging in the centre and tapered at the ends. Dark and shiny. *Leeches!*

I'd never experienced a leech in person, but I had read about them in my medical textbooks. Hirudin, a compound extracted from leeches, is an anticoagulant that can dissolve blood clots. At least, I knew they weren't venomous, but they could be difficult to extract from the skin. I didn't want to do it myself, and I was pretty sure Len would freak out if I asked him to do it. I'd have to wait for Ram to arrive and hope he was proficient in external parasite removal.

I went outside in the faint blue-grey light of dawn and tried various manoeuvres to get them off my body without touching them. First, I shook my legs. They didn't budge. Then I tried jumping up and down. No luck. I hummed loudly, creating inner vibrations in my body that I hoped would disturb them. They didn't care. In my estimation, they were growing by the minute. Maybe all the hopping around increased my blood flow and fed them faster. *Damn it!*

I decided to be discreet about the new turn of events. If we had any chance of getting out of there as a group, I had to remain silent about the wretched things. It would be difficult enough to convince the group to take the journey. They didn't need to know about the parasites. At breakfast, I sat far away from everyone else as if I had a contagious skin condition. I was a leper colony of one.

I spoke to Len as soon as he woke up and suggested that while trying to sell the trekking rescue option, we should leave out the most dangerous elements. Instead, we should focus on Ram's intimate knowledge of the area, the confidence of the commander, the tasty food packets, and the short flight to safety. Since Len, who was one of the oldest members of the group, could make the trip, I figured anyone could.

Meanwhile, Marilyn was anxious to hear what Len and I had to say. We gathered everyone in the dining hall and shared our information. Surprisingly, Marilyn listened attentively along with the rest of the group. I glossed over a few of the specifics, such as the rotting log bridge, the dirt wall, the landslides, the sheer drop-offs, and the narrow outcroppings—but I also made sure they knew it wasn't going to be easy. Len had already decided he would be leaving the following day. I would be going as well.

Marilyn approached me after my speech. Her expression offered no clue as to what was going through her mind.

"What do you think?" I asked.

"I agree we should leave on foot. I see few other options. We're low on food, and everyone's patience is wearing thin. Once we get to a safer place, we will regroup and again go into silence." She stated it as if the retreat could somehow be salvaged. I knew better, but I didn't challenge her idea.

I informed Marilyn about the possibility of the smallest helicopter being able to land for Sarah since she had a broken foot. Marilyn jumped on the information and promised to make arrangements. She then told everyone to get ready to leave the following day. Suddenly, my plan that she had resisted for so long became her idea, her baby. And she was right back where she was most comfortable—telling people what to do.

BJ was the first to complain. He loathed the idea of having to walk so far and suggested an alternative.

"What do you have in mind?" I asked him.

"Well, those who welcome the pain from a six-hour hike should go right ahead," he snapped. "But the rest of us should be allowed to stay here until they can come get us."

"That might work. If you don't mind waiting a few weeks and hope they can air-drop some food in the meantime. Talk to Marilyn. She's the boss." I replied, turning to leave. I was done listening to him.

I joined Len in our room. He was watching our roommates hastily grab all the belongings they had brought to the retreat. "The commander at the camp told us large bags won't be

197

allowed. Only personal items," Len reminded them. They ignored him and continued to pack.

Giving up, Len sauntered outside, shaking his head. I was right behind him. "I don't get it, Niranjan. Why aren't they listening?"

"I honestly don't know," I replied. "Do they really think they're going to be able to drag their luggage over the mountain?" I entertained the thought for a minute—an entire line of hikers from a spiritual retreat, dragging their jumbo suitcases and duffle bags behind them. It was too much for me. I burst out laughing, and soon Len was howling along with me. The entire idea was too absurd.

Ram arrived later that morning looking fresh and eager for more work. I had paid him well for his work the day before. It was only about ten American dollars, but in India, that was a decent day's wage. I ushered Ram aside and beckoned him to follow me. I hurried behind the main building, away from the sight of bystanders, and pulled up the bottoms of my scrub pants.

He gave me a head bobble and a smile and got to work immediately. He could have been a surgeon if he had been properly educated and trained. He unhitched one end of a leech by pinching my skin with the fingers of his left hand while using the thumbnail to detach the sucker. Then he did the same with the other end. Before the leech could dig back in, he deftly flicked it into the bushes. It was far enough away that I would never see it again. Suddenly, it made sense why the fingernail on his left thumb was left long while the rest were trimmed. It came in handy as a leech removing tool.

I jumped up and down and jogged in place to make sure all the remnants had fallen off. Ram did such a superb job that there was barely any trace. I had envisioned a gory scene. I couldn't remember how many times I thanked him for various things, not the least of which was liberation from leech infestation. He was my hero for too many reasons. How could I ever repay him for everything he'd done for me?

Marilyn wanted more specifics from Ram once he arrived, so I snagged Len for backup, and the three of us went to find her. Once a firm decision had been made to leave the next day, there was a palpable shift in the mood. We passed a young woman who was methodically laying ropes on the ground. Two long pieces ran parallel, and several short pieces ran across at intervals of roughly one foot.

"What's she doing?" Ram asked.

"It looks like a rope ladder to me," I replied. The young woman heard me and proudly showed me the first knot she had tied. It looked complicated and held firm as she tugged on the two ropes that were then married together. She said she was an amateur climber and was making the rope ladder so people could hold onto it and walk as a group.

Ram looked gravely concerned and then let out a short laugh. "Please, tell madam, no ropes. If one slips, everyone falls." He was spot on. Not to mention, the trail twisted and turned so often, there were very few places her creation would be able to unfold in one straight line. Those were the places it was easiest to walk without any kind of support.

I relayed Ram's Hindi message to the young woman, but she ignored us and continued to work on her ladder. I wasted no more breath. If she had climbing experience, as soon as she got onto the mountain, it would become apparent to her that Ram was correct.

We spotted Marilyn sitting on a chair at the highest point on the ashram grounds, keeping an eye on everyone. I told her I would translate for Ram. It would be beneficial to have a buffer in between. If Marilyn sounded a little rough, I could smooth the edges of her words. Ram was beyond precious and deserved all the respect we could muster.

"I've made arrangements for the small helicopter to attempt a pick up for Sarah tomorrow morning," Marilyn announced.

"Excellent!" I replied. "Ram thinks he can round up enough locals to provide one helper for each of the group members. I think it would be extremely beneficial for us. The locals are used to navigating the rough terrain and can focus on one person to advice and assist."

"Yes," replied Marilyn thoughtfully. "And they will be able to carry the luggage as well."

"Luggage?" I couldn't believe what I was hearing. "No, no one is taking the luggage. It won't be allowed on the helicopters."

"Well, I'm not sure everyone would be agreeable to leaving their things behind. Let me find out."

Marilyn strode down the hill and called everyone together for an impromptu meeting in the dining hall. She explained the situation. A surprising number of people flat out refused to leave unless their bags went with them. The general complaint was that if we were to continue the retreat at another location, people would need their extra clothing, meditation accessories, and other belongings. They also had in their minds that, since they were foreigners with evacuation priority, the rule of no luggage wouldn't apply to them. Len and I stared at each other in disbelief.

Marilyn concluded the meeting by declaring, "Okay, don't worry. We will find a way to send your luggage with you."

Back outside, Ram and I met once more with Marilyn. Ram said it would be impossible to manage luggage and people.

"Maybe we could send the bags ahead of time?" she suggested.

"Exactly how do you propose to do that?" I envisioned tossing all the bags in the river and letting them float downstream to the dam. It was very satisfying.

"Ram, of course. His guys will manage."

"Manage what, Marilyn?" I was beyond trying to hide my annoyance.

"The luggage leaves this afternoon. Have Ram bring some of his guys now. I will make calls and find a safe place to store the bags for the night."

I asked Ram in Hindi if that would work. I promised I would haggle with Marilyn to get a very fair price for all his time and trouble. He agreed. Ram suggested a thousand rupees per head for providing the individual assistants for the trek the next day, which was about thirteen dollars per person. There were forty-four of us. I told Marilyn that was quite reasonable, but she insisted on paying thirty-five thousand for everyone, or about ten dollars each. Ram reluctantly agreed, and then Marilyn had the nerve to ask Ram if he and his friends would consider making the extra trip with the luggage as part of the already agreed-upon price. He refused. He wanted extra for dealing with people's stupidity. I didn't blame him one bit. Marilyn agreed to pay ten thousand additional rupees, about one hundred and thirty dollars, for carrying close to a hundred bags. Then came the question of responsibility. Ram refused, understandably, to be responsible for the bags once they got to the other side. Who would guard them? Where would they put them?

I asked Ram to go back to his village and return with reinforcements.

Marilyn somehow managed to get in touch with the dam operator through her growing web of contacts. They agreed to give us a room in their guest house. Apparently, they had comfortable accommodations for visiting engineers and senior management. Due to the floods, it was empty and locked, and the keys were at the local police station a couple of miles farther downstream from the dam. Marilyn volunteered Len and me to accompany Ram and the hundred-odd bags that were scheduled to leave that afternoon.

"Okay," I agreed. "We'll go down with the bags, but I want to stay overnight in the guesthouse."

"You can't do that. You have to return tonight so you can walk with us tomorrow."

"You're kidding! That's an extra twelve hours of hiking!"

"I don't care. You must come back."

I couldn't decide if she was evil or clueless, but it didn't matter. The result was the same. I wanted to scream until she melted into the ground. Instead, I walked away. I sat outside with Len for a while until I calmed down. Then I managed to convince myself it would be better to spend eighteen hours walking back and forth over the mountains because that meant eighteen hours less I would have to be near Marilyn. *In two days, this will be over*, I told myself. *Be patient. This is a spiritual test.*

Chapter 24

Shortly after lunch, Ram returned with fifteen strong and sturdy villagers. He reassured us there would be more helpers available for the hike out the following day, but they had already committed to repairing trails that afternoon. Undaunted by the mammoth heap of luggage in front of them, Ram and his crew got to work immediately. With great efficiency, they sorted the bags by weight and size. I quickly calculated they would have to carry about six each. As I began to worry that might not be possible, Ram declared they would make two trips. That meant Len and I would wait at the dam with the luggage while the other guys returned for the rest. That was fine with me. I couldn't wait to get away from the crowd around us. People were jostling each other in order to stuff last-minute items into their suitcases, and others were yanking things out. Ram quickly grew impatient and demanded no more fiddling with the bags.

Each of the porters made a personal cargo net by tying together thick ropes of jute. Then, they fashioned three loops on each net—one for each shoulder, and one to anchor around their foreheads. Ram expertly loaded the nets and situated the bundles on everyone's backs. As soon as all the loads were secure, Ram's men hurried off in the direction of the dam.

Before we left, Len gave me a couple of ibuprofen tablets along with some mysterious herbal medicine pills. The ibuprofen successfully dulled my muscle and joint pains from the previous day's adventure. I'm not sure what the other pills were for, but they took up a little space in my stomach, for which I was grateful. I wasn't certain when or what we would eat next.

Len and I clumsily helped Ram get his load strapped to his back. It occurred to me then that I should refer to him as a sherpa instead of a porter. That was a more respectable term. From then on, I began to address him as Sherpa Ram. It made him giggle, which made me happy. I felt somewhat guilty for not shouldering a share of the weight, but it would be more than enough work to get myself there and back safely. Ram and the other men were in much better shape than I. Len didn't feel right about not carrying anything as well. He chose to allay his guilt by leaving his suitcase behind. I did the same with my rucksack.

The three of us set off briskly into the woods. It was much easier to keep up with Ram when he was weighed down with a hundred extra pounds. All of the other guys had long disappeared from view. They were far ahead of us. Though they were transporting a heavy burden, they didn't have the added responsibility of safely guiding Len and me. I was determined not to allow the leeches to get me again. I pulled my hiking socks up as far as possible and tucked my scrub bottoms deep into them. I hoped it would suffice as a barrier.

The hike went much more smoothly the second time around. It helped that I knew what dangers lay ahead on the trail. I also recognised certain landmarks along the way that indicated how much farther we had to go. Showing great foresight, Ram had brought along a couple of plastic stools. He stacked one on top of the other to help us get up the slippery dirt wall, then left them there for all of us to use again. The prolonged steep incline was just as challenging as the day before, but the two rotting logs that spanned the enormous gap had been reinforced. I remembered the logs being a little loose the previous night on our way back. They were definitely more secure that morning. Perhaps the other sherpas had paused and reworked them to ensure they would hold the extra weight and increased traffic.

When we were about halfway to the dam, we encountered the men jogging towards us empty-handed. They had already reached the other side of the river, left the bags with one person, and were returning for the second load. It was an impressive physical feat to trek across once with such heavy loads, but to do it again, and so quickly? In my opinion, those guys were woefully underpaid.

Marilyn had told our group, after her haggling session with Ram, that we were not to tip the men separately once we all reached safely. In reply, Len had said, "Screw that!" He was planning to give Ram and the other men several thousand rupees, or whatever Indian money was leftover in his fanny pack. My cash was sitting in solidarity with his in that bulging sack of leather. I had no objections to paying them much more than initially agreed upon. Their help was invaluable. Marilyn completely failed to consider that fact during her haggling, but no matter. She need not know what Len and I planned to do.

Watching the men rush by, fully dedicated to the task at hand, provided me with a minuscule yet much-needed infusion of positivity and motivation. Admittedly, resentment and negativity had been festering in my mind since leaving the retreat centre. Even though I wasn't carrying a load, I was feeling bitter about being sent along to take the luggage. I suspected it was because Marilyn didn't trust the men not to steal anything, but I knew they were honest people. They had no interest in taking anyone's meditation accessories and Western clothing. They only wanted the money we had offered. Besides, how was I going to stop anyone from taking anything if I wasn't actually with them? Mostly, though, I was angry about Marilyn insisting Len and I return that night solely for her peace of mind. We were demanding so much of our bodies, risking life and limb to cross the mountains for the sake of replaceable material possessions. The rest of the group members were probably spending their day gossiping, relaxing, and sipping watered-down tea.

I was growing quite tired by the time we reached the grassy patch that had suffered blows from falling rocks in one of the landslides. The boulder I had rested on the previous day was still in place. I was tempted to take a break. Even Ram seemed to be slowing down at that point. The suitcases bulging through the net were nothing but meaningless deadweight. My anger at Marilyn and the others who refused to leave without their bags was beginning to fester in me again. I tried to keep my focus on the ground in front of me as we did our best to hurry on, wasting no time. The plan was to get back to the ashram by sunset, but I knew that was overly optimistic.

Twist after turn, rise after fall, we pushed on until we came to the part of the trail that followed high along the river, the dam finally within reach. I could hear Len starting to stumble behind me from exhaustion. I prayed he wouldn't trip and fall down into the water below. Once at the dam, we were able to rest while waiting for the remaining bags to arrive. I wasn't entirely sure why Ram didn't multitask and look for the police station during that time, but I didn't raise the issue with him. I was exhausted and thankful to be sitting down.

As soon as the sherpas made it back, Len, Ram, and I let them take a turn to rest while we continued on a couple of miles in the direction of the police station. It turned out to be impossible to locate. The building, and the ground it had been sitting on, were somewhere downstream. Where the new riverbank had formed, the police department had erected a large tent. When we entered, it was empty except for a long folding table with a cracked wooden top. It was propped up by crooked metal legs. Two officers sat behind the table in matching rusted folding chairs, one of them puffing on a cigarette and holding a worn leather binder in front of him. I wondered if it was some sort of important record book— perhaps the one thing they were able to save from the crumbling building before the flood took everything else.

I guessed the smoking officer was the one in charge based on the fact that he was holding the last remaining bit of the police station. I apprised him that we were from the meditation centre upstream and were there to pick up a key to the house by the dam. He questioned me repeatedly, uncertain as to whether I was the victim of a crime or a potential perpetrator of one. He peppered me with questions while eying Ram with suspicion and Len with curiosity. It was only when I mentioned the luggage waiting by the dam that he had the information he needed to grant us access to the guesthouse. He readily handed me the keys and pointed at the sky. In the general direction of his finger was a road that went straight up a long, steep hill.

Ram's men were unhappy to hear about the turn of events that would require them to haul the luggage a significant distance to yet a higher elevation. Fearing a mutiny that would leave Len, Ram, and me to transport all the bags up to the guesthouse, I offered to buy refreshments for everyone at the nearest tea stall. The elderly roadside vendor stooped over his small pushcart, boiling a large pot of tea on a kerosene stove. His hands quivered as he served up a thick, milky brew that left a lingering bitterness of over-steeped tea leaves. Along with the drink, he served vegetables that had been dipped in lentil batter, then fried in oil until golden brown and crisp. I squeezed the excess oil out of my serving before popping it in my mouth. The traditional Indian tea break was exactly what we all needed. The grumbling within the ranks dissipated, and we returned to the luggage on the dam, prepared to carry it up the long hill.

From our position, we could easily see the heavy wrought iron gate at the bottom of the hill, blocking off the private road to the guesthouse somewhere on top. There was also a stone wall that wound around the perimeter of the property. What we didn't see until we arrived at the gate was that it was locked with an oversized padlock. We had one small key, and it was definitely not for the gate. Len tried it anyway, but the giant keyhole effortlessly swallowed the useless piece of metal. The gate was over six feet tall and had sharp spikes protruding at the top. There was no way to safely climb over it.

Since the local police knew who we were, Len had no qualms about pulling himself up onto the five-foot wall next to the gate. He quickly discovered it would not be a simple matter of jumping down to the other side and handing the bags over. There was thick undergrowth and a dense hedge along the wall, presumably to prevent trespassers. I thought of all the snakes that might be hiding there and knew the bushes were officially off-limits. A few of us teetered along the top of the wall and found a clear spot to jump down.

With all the protections set in place, I expected to encounter a mansion hidden at the top of the hill. Instead, I found a small two-room house. We unlocked the door, swollen with moisture, and tugged it open. The musty air inside was grateful to escape. The front room was empty except for a bed and a side table. We would put all of the luggage there.

As Len and I walked down to the gate, Ram's men were already at work, tossing over suitcases and duffle bags. Each one landed with a dull thud. Fortunately, none of them broke open and spilled their contents on the road.

When the last of the luggage was put away and the key safely in Len's possession, we all crossed back over the dam. It was late afternoon at that point, and as soon as we hit the trail, all of the men took off running. They knew only one speed to get home: fast.

Ram, Len, and I trekked back over the ridges and through the forest in the late afternoon light. We were still walking when the sun settled below the horizon, so Ram donned my headlamp. He asked if he could keep it, and since the elastic had been washed with his sweat, I made no arguments against his request. Ram patiently guided us back to the ashram, step by step. I was thankful we had no incidents or falls. It was past 9:00 p.m. when we emerged from the trees, dragging our feet, and crossed the boundary of the ashram. That time, we were accorded a hero's welcome. Marilyn, BJ, and Guru Ananda were nowhere in sight, but everyone else stood on either side of the path leading to the dining hall. They were clapping, patting us on the back, and singing our praises. After all, we had saved their luggage.

Chapter 25

It felt like checkout time after a leisurely week at a resort. Everyone was animatedly talking over each other, laughing and joking as if we hadn't almost met death mere days before. Some were posing for pictures by the river. Others were exchanging phone numbers and email addresses to keep in touch. Marilyn had been trying to assure people the retreat would continue once we reached safety, but they seemed to know better. Everyone was focused on getting back home. Most of the group members held purses or small daypacks and wore hats and sunglasses.

I hadn't seen Guru Ananda for a couple of days. Soon enough, though, he emerged from his room. Instead of his ochre robes, he wore bright orange sweatpants and a matching T-shirt. His sweatpants were neatly tucked into his white socks, which were pulled high. A pair of black New Balance sneakers completed his stylish ensemble. He was ready to go. BJ and Marilyn, on the other hand, did not look ready at all. BJ was wearing his white dhoti and a pair of sandals. It occurred to me that he might not have anything appropriate to wear for the demanding hike, but what about Marilyn? I knew she had suitable clothing, yet she was dressed in her white sari. There was no way she could trek in that.

Ram appeared with over forty villagers, one to assist each group member along the trail. He matched up the pairs at random, then made rounds to provide each person with a crude walking stick fashioned from tree branches. Since Len and I were experienced with the hike, we decided to share Ram between us. Marilyn passed around the collection bowl, each of us chipping in our bit of the money to pay for the personal mountain guides.

The sound of helicopters flying overhead had been constant the last couple of days, so I thought nothing of another one until I realised it was heading straight for us. As it approached, it slowly began to make wide circles. Sarah's helicopter. The commander had kept his promise to send one to pick her up. It was one of the small ones. I saw one pilot. I wondered if it had two seats or four. It lowered slowly, the pilot carefully eying the ground below. As it descended, it kicked up sand, dirt, and leaves, and blew a few hats off people's heads. Its two skids settled gently on the sandy riverbank, which provided just enough soggy ground to land. The pilot kept the rotors running. Marilyn ran to the helicopter, crouching low and shielding her hair with her sari. I couldn't hear what she was saying to the pilot, but she was clearly trying to yell over the noise. I could see the jugular veins popping in her neck.

BJ gallantly assisted Sarah to her ride. I was impressed by the thoughtful act. He gently helped her into one of the back seats. Without hesitation, Marilyn climbed into the other back seat, and BJ jumped in front. I couldn't believe it. For all Marilyn's talk about sticking together as a group, she was abandoning us at the first offer of an easy way out. I was livid. Len and I had spent a full twenty-four hours out of the last forty-eight tromping through hell to arrange to get everyone to safety. In my opinion, the proper thing to do would have been for Marilyn to offer for Len and me to fly out with Sarah. After all, we were suffering from debilitating body aches and crippling exhaustion. Yet, I was positive the thought had never occurred to her.

The pilot tried to lift off, but the helicopter didn't respond. The sand under the skids was extremely wet, and he had sunk into the ground. In a moment of satisfying karmic retribution, the pilot offloaded BJ. Only then was he able to successfully ascend.

BJ grudgingly returned to the group, mumbling some excuse about needing to fly out because of his back. Guru Ananda gave him a hardy slap on the back. I couldn't tell if it was in appreciation of BJ joining us or in reprimand for his attempt to sneak away. Either way, the guru's smile never left his face. BJ was holding his huge black backpack. He proudly stated that every single thing he owned was in that bag and then pawned it off on one of the helpers.

The villagers looked anxious to get going as everyone stood around, taking their final pictures with the new friends they had made. When it came time for a single group photo, several group members refused to participate. They didn't want to be in the same picture frame with others with whom they had squabbled and disagreed. Len shot me a look. I rolled my eyes. Thankfully, Guru Ananda stepped forward and declared we should get going, which set the slow train to safety in motion.

The final time across would be my fifth. I figured that gave me the right to go ahead of everyone else on the expedition. The others would be walking at their own pace with their chaperones, so I had no responsibilities or uncertainties to deal with. I was free to enjoy the flowing thought of imminent freedom. Len had forgotten to give the key to Marilyn, which also justified us going ahead of the group. She would have landed by then and would have to wait in the hot sun for several hours for the rest of us to join her.

The stools that Ram had stacked at the first major obstacle, the mud wall, made it easy to climb over. My clothes were already soiled. I hadn't bathed or shaved in days. I wholeheartedly embraced the wall for the last time and kissed the mud that was peeling off. Somewhere in the back of my mind, I promised myself that I would return one day with Len to visit our hero Ram and make sure life was treating him properly.

The sun was shining intensely. The air was fresh. The sky held not a single cloud in her embrace. Ram hummed as we walked, undoubtedly feeling lighter that his role as a saviour was almost over. As we conquered the steep incline and the rotting log bridge for the last time, I wondered how well the other group members would navigate the obstacles. With every forward step, I imagined Marilyn receding from a rear-view mirror. It was very gratifying. My mind began to wander back to my home, to my family, while my feet marched around the hairpin turns—step, step, step, *whoosh*.

The trail crumbled beneath me.

Before I could form a thought, my hands shot out to grab something—anything—as I found myself dangling below the edge. Ram turned and lunged for my arm that was miraculously attached to a tree root by the sheer will of one hand. I glanced down to see how far I would fall if I let go, and all I saw was my certain end. My other hand reached up and fumbled along the ground, desperately clutching loose earth that crumbled with each grasp. Ram crouched down in a half-squat and yelled for Len to hold onto him. Len crouched as well, placed his arms around Ram, and leaned back to keep them both from tumbling off the side of the mountain. Ram dug his bare toes into the ground, and he and Len both heaved backwards with a coordinated pull. I could do nothing to help, but at least I had the presence of mind not to struggle. Ram dragged me back up onto the trail with pure brute strength, and the three of us collapsed in a heap on the ground.

"Sir," pleaded Ram from the middle layer of the heap. "Please do not do that again."

"Okay," I promised.

Despite our mishap and the resulting reduction of our speed, we were the first ones to arrive at the dam. We waited as the others trickled in, pair by pair. Each time someone else emerged from the trees, the rest of us would clap. That went on for a couple of hours, all the while standing on the dam's road and watching. The heat of the summer sun bore down on the black asphalt, and my mouth was parched, but I stayed with the others. BJ was the last to emerge. His dhoti and shirt were stained with mud. He had obviously fallen somewhere along the way—likely more than once. He appeared to be in real pain. I felt a flutter of sympathy and silently forgave him for trying to hitch a ride on the helicopter.

Marilyn was presumably waiting for us farther downriver at the field station, so everyone looked to Len and me for further instructions. I suggested we first go retrieve the luggage that was up the hill in the guesthouse, but the villagers refused to move another inch until they were paid for getting everyone safely to the dam. Transporting the bags from the guesthouse had not been included in the original agreement, so we had to renegotiate the terms. Since the money for the villagers was with Marilyn, Len passed around his hat and collected whatever extra money people were willing to pay for the bag retrieval. Ram convinced his crew to bring the bags down the hill to the dam, and the group members would take everything from there. Len and I slipped a thick wad of rupees to Ram and asked him to distribute it as a tip among the villagers after they were done. We were eternally grateful for all of their help.

The villagers tossed the bags over the locked gate onto the road and carried them a couple at a time to the dam. That's where they stopped. Ram was anxious about the money Marilyn had promised him, so Len went with him to the camp and retrieved the money from Marilyn. When they returned, the group members were facing off with the villagers. People were once more complaining about having to drag their own bags over the broken road the rest of the way to the field station. Ram was able to convince a handful of his men to help, and I picked up the suitcases of two of our group members who were hurting from the unforgiving hike. BJ thrust his backpack into my chest. "Take this too," he snapped.

Together, we painstakingly pulled our embattled train up to its final stop at the camp. We had officially arrived—all of us victorious—into the clearing where the helicopters were landing.

Like the previous days, on the far side of the clearing were refugees waiting in the sun. Only there were thousands more. Most of them were completely empty-handed. Marilyn was on the near side of the field, standing under a shaded canopy with several military men. As we were still dragging our luggage behind us, a soldier ushered us under the canopy. A second soldier passed out food packets and bottles of water. While I was mindlessly wolfing down the food and water, a commander came to speak to our group.

"There can be no bags!" he barked in English, motioning to our things. "These pilots are risking their own lives to get everyone down from the mountains safely. We are making room on the helicopters for people, not luggage! Only small, necessary items."

Upon hearing the words of the commander and seeing thousands of people waiting patiently in the sun to fly to safety, something must have clicked within the group. Surprisingly, I didn't hear anyone argue. They simply began to dig through their suitcases for the most important items they could stuff into their purses and small daypacks. So much for all the fuss over the stupid bags. It was all for nothing. Absolutely nothing. Like a little kid, I wanted to scream, "I told you so!" But instead, I simply reminded myself it was a spiritual test.

Massive military helicopters were landing and taking off at regular intervals. Designed for troop transport, they could accommodate twenty people or more. The ITBP commander allowed Marilyn to put two of our people on each flight, and any remaining seats were assigned to those waiting in the sun. Each time one of the helicopters landed, Marilyn rushed under the canopy and chose who to send away. Guru Ananda and BJ were the first to go.

Anyone in line to board had to prove their possessions were essential. Despite everything, a young woman from our group tried to take her suitcase. One of the soldiers demanded that she leave it behind. When she argued with him, he snatched her bag, unzipped it, and dumped its contents onto the ground. She wailed as the desperate and impatient people in line behind her shoved her towards the waiting chopper.

The crowd under the canopy was thinning little by little. Len was in no hurry to go. He was busy chatting with Gretchen, for who knew how many more lifetimes would pass before they met again. Another helicopter landed. The turnaround was swift, five to ten minutes at most. Since Len and Gretchen were standing near the entrance, Marilyn grabbed them and told them to hurry up and board. They strolled hand in hand as if they had no worries. Gretchen's light blonde hair danced in the wind, catching dust kicked up by the rotor blades. Suddenly Marilyn had a change of heart. She yelled for Gretchen to come back, then pushed me into the group of people waiting to board.

Since Len was already at the head of the line, I joined him there. I was the first one on board and snagged a seat on the end of a long bench—by the window, no less. I was ecstatic. The two bench seats were facing each other. Len sat across from me, in front of the other window. People continued to pile inside until every spot was filled. As soon as the last person was seated, a soldier closed the door, and we gently lifted off, one step closer to home.

A young man and his father sat next to me. They were pilgrims from southern India and spoke the native language from my home state of Karnataka. They detailed the misery they endured during their journey to the camp. They went without food for the three days it took them to trek to the evacuation point. They were close to Gangotri when the flooding began and told me about the tens of thousands of people stranded in different parts of that area. They estimated thousands of people died, some instantly, carried away by mud and water. Bridges and roads were decimated, and tens of thousands must have been rendered homeless. His account of the destruction was similar to what Marilyn had heard through updates on the satellite phone. Hearing his words, I had a difficult time wrapping my mind around the magnitude of the damage.

The helicopter bobbed side to side as if being gently cradled. We soared into the air, making wide, sweeping circles. I could see the ashram in the distance and thought I saw a hint of the SOS sign Len and I had made. The people below us, waiting for their chance to be rescued, turned into tiny specks as we rose higher and cleared the mountain in front of us.

We flew above the river, following it south. The man to my left said we would be landing at a temporary army base that was set up as a refugee camp for tens of thousands of people. From there, we would eventually be put on military trucks and driven somewhere else. Shortly thereafter, the camp came into view. There was a long, straight clearing that looked like a runway. Numerous tents were visible on either side, set in straight lines of about twenty tents each. There were at least twenty helicopters on the runway, waiting to take off. We circled overhead. As our pilot spoke into his microphone, I could see his lips move, but I couldn't hear what was being said. He looked very professional and capable in his smart blue uniform with the Indian Air Force insignia prominently displayed on the sleeve. His gold-rimmed Ray-Ban aviator sunglasses gave him a bit of Bollywood flair.

We circled around the camp for about fifteen minutes. At one point, we descended to a lower altitude where the people on the ground looked like action figure toys. The air traffic controllers must not have cleared the pilot to land because suddenly, the helicopter jerked to the side and rose again. As we flew away from the camp, people began to clap. I asked the man next to me what was happening. He said since we didn't land at the base, it meant we would be flying directly to the airport at Dehradun. It was a city at the base of the Himalayas, relatively close to Haridwar. With that information, I knew we had bypassed the enormous hurdle of waiting several days in the military base for a ride out. Len and I smiled at each other as we realised our good fortune.

I had a clear view of the full force that had been unleashed on the surrounding mountains. Most of them were completely bare, heavily marked with the long, broad streaks of landslides in every direction. The main highway was covered in landslides in many different places, with cars stopped on the cracked areas between them. It would take a monumental effort to rescue all those people and restore road access. We continued downstream along the river, and I could see that most of the massive steel bridges that spanned the water had lost their entire middle sections. We flew over Rishikesh, where the giant statue of Shiva was chest-deep in water.

After about an hour and a half of flying, we finally emerged from the mountains. I was overcome with relief to see flat, open land again. Before long, the airport in Dehradun was below us. The helicopter circled a few times, and we were given permission to land. Once we touched down, I felt all of the stress I had been harbouring the past few days shift into low gear. I couldn't remember another time in my life I had been so utterly finished. So hungry, so filthy, so exhausted, so sore. As soon as the helicopter door opened, Army medics with first aid kits ushered us into the terminal building. They checked everyone over, making sure no one needed medical attention.

"Are you injured? Dehydrated?" one of the medics asked us.

"We'll be okay," I replied, "but we got separated from our group. Do you know how I can make a phone call to let them know we are okay?"

The medic allowed us to use his mobile to contact Marilyn on the satellite phone.

"Where are you?" she demanded.

"We landed at the airport in Dehradun." I spoke loudly so she could hear me over all the noise on her end.

"You need to come back!" she exclaimed.

"What do you mean? Len and I are safe. From here, we can fly anywhere we need to go."

"We need to stick together as a group! They are telling us it will take several days for us to get the rest of the way down the mountain since the bridges are out. You need to stay with us!"

"Nope. There's no way that'll happen, Marilyn. Sorry. Bye!" I yelled and hung up the phone. "Thank you," I told the medic as I handed his phone back.

"No problem, sir. Please stay here until the officials can take your names and important information. Then you are free to go."

"Niranjan!" Len exclaimed. "You just said no to Marilyn!" He patted me on the back. "I'm proud of you. How did it feel?"

221

"It felt amazing, actually," I replied.

The two of us collapsed in a couple of chairs and just looked at each other.

"It's over," I said carefully, not wanting to jinx anything.

"Yeah, it's over," Len echoed. He smiled. "What a ride!"

"Unforgettable."

"What are you gonna do now?" Len asked. "I think I might go check out the Taj Mahal."

I laughed. "I have no plans to go anywhere near death for a while."

"How do you mean?" Len asked, puzzled.

"You know the Taj Mahal is a tomb, right? An extraordinarily beautiful, gigantic tomb."

"Huh," replied Len. "You don't say."

"I'm going to stop in Bangalore and visit my parents," I continued. "I could really use some of my mom's home cooking. I plan to lie on the couch in my dad's study and listen to all the Beethoven he wants." I couldn't think of anything that would make him happier. Or me. And I couldn't think of a more welcome time in my life to hear 'Ode to Joy'.

After speaking to the officer, we were led outside the terminal. It was a scene of chaos. News outlets were interviewing refugees. Community groups were distributing hot food and cash to the survivors who had nothing left to their names. Len was the only Westerner in sight, and a TV news crew seized him for an interview. Microphones were shoved up to his face, and questions spilled out from every surrounding mouth. He winked at me, completely in his element.

"Where are you from?"

"What did you see from the helicopter?"

"Can you describe your rescue?"

"What was it like to experience the Himalayan tsunami?"

The TV screen on the wall behind Len was showing aerial photos and clips of the aftermath. The news ticker scrolling at the bottom repeatedly flashed the extraordinarily high number of expected fatalities and missing people. At that moment, it occurred to me that a natural disaster of that proportion had probably been picked up by American news stations. My heart sank as I thought of my wife assuming my worst possible fate from the news. I hastily borrowed another phone from a random passer-by so I could call her and let her know I was okay.

I dialled, praying she would pick up. I needed to hear her voice, tell her I was safe. It was the middle of the night back home. I hoped she was sleeping soundly, but if she had any knowledge of what was happening, she'd be wide awake.

"Hello?" She answered on the first ring.

"Hey, sweet angel."

"My God. You're alive."

Printed in the USA
CPSIA information can be obtained
at www.ICGtesting.com
LVHW020821151023
760911LV00064B/1176

9 781528 968911